MEDITERRANEAN COOKING

Mediterranean cooking, so "poor" and yet so rich, captures the flavors of the sun and the sea, of pasta and olive oil, of basil and hot red pepper, of simplicity and genuineness. It is a straightforward and natural cuisine, inviting and richly-scented, lighthearted and colorful, based on not very elaborate dishes that generally require little cooking time. It is a cuisine that prefers fats of vegetable origin, like light and flavorful extra virgin olive oil, golden or green. Nutritionists have for some time now acknowledged the healthful qualities of olive oil, a basic element in the "Mediterranean diet," the regime most suitable not only for those who want to slough off excess poundage but also for those who want to keep in shape – and healthy. It is a summertime cuisine, in all senses: low in calories and thus perfect for the warm months, but at the same time capable of enlivening the table with sunny flavors and solar emotions even in the darkest months, when a plate of spaghetti, topped with a little olive oil, a sprig of basil, and fresh tomato (now fortunately available all year round), is all that's needed to bring to mind – and to the palate – all the joyous sensations of the year's best season.

Most of our recipes are illustrated with sequences of photographs showing the different steps in preparation, especially "when a picture is worth a thousand words." As usual, the list of ingredients does not include table salt and pepper, since they are taken for granted in Italian cooking like the water used for cooking pasta or boiling various foods. Listing them would only be time and space wasted (but in all the recipes, the right time to add these seasonings – preferably with moderation – is indicated). Salt is included only in the ingredient lists for sweets and cookies, where it is used sparingly and then not always. We suggest reading the ingredients carefully (along with the information on preparation and cooking times, the level of difficulty, the more or less accentuated flavor, and nutritional information) and then reading the recipe through before beginning. And, as usual . . . bon appetit !

FROM THE OLIVE TO OIL

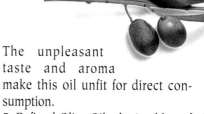

• The olive tree, whether tall and leafy or slender and twisted, has been a constant in the Mediterranean basin since time immemorial, the common denominator in the landscapes of such different areas as Italy, France's Provence and Spain, Greece and Turkey, North Africa (and in particular Tunisia), and the Middle East. From its modest and yet choice fruits we press a unique condiment, pure olive oil. The look of the olive trees, the flavor of the fruit and the oil, and its aroma and acidity all differ considerably from area to area of production; the oil of the central Mediterranean is generally the most highly valued.

• The olives (fleshy fruits or drupes) turn from green to blackish violet as they ripen. Of variable forms and sizes, the fruits are broadly classified as "table" and "oil" varieties. The table olives, generally selected among those varieties with the largest fruits, are preserved in brines of different types, treated with lime and caustic soda, or oven-dried. The so-called *conciate* olives are flavored with herbs (garlic, fennel, oregano, hot red pepper, thyme, etc.).

• Olive oil is a fat (liquid at room temperature), obtained by crushing and pressing olives, which is separated from the pomace (solid residue) and the residual moisture. At 15°C/59°F, its density is 0.916 and its specific weight 916 g/l. It is unequaled in the kitchen, whether used raw as a dressing or for cooking. It is excellent above all for frying (even though it is normally replaced, for this use, by the less expensive corn oil) because the antioxidant action exerted by is components makes it resistant to high temperatures – and this means that unhealthful substances are freed only much later than by other oils, or not at all, at the temperatures generally reached in the kitchen.

• The international classification published by the International Olive Oil Council (IOOC), which counts 96% of the world's olive-growing countries among its members, divides olive oil into the different categories listed below.
1. Virgin Extra or Extra Virgin Olive Oil (free acidity, expressed as oleic acid, of not more than 1%).
2. Virgin Olive Oil (acidity not exceeding 2%).
3. Ordinary Virgin Olive Oil (acidity not exceeding 3.3%).
4. Lampante Virgin Olive Oil (acidity exceeding 3.3%).

The unpleasant taste and aroma make this oil unfit for direct consumption.
5. Refined Olive Oil, obtained by refining virgin olive oils, not including lampante (acidity 0.5%).
6. Olive Oil, obtained by mixing refined olive oil and virgin olive oils, not including lampante (acidity 1.5%)
7. Crude Olive-Pomace Oil, obtained by treating olive pomace (residual olive pulp after pressing of the virgin oils) with solvents. This oil is inedible as is.
8. Refined Olive-Pomace Oil, obtained by refining crude olive-pomace oil (acidity 0.5%). This oil is inedible as is.
9. Olive-Pomace Oil, oil that consists of a mixture of refined olive-pomace oil and virgin olive oils, not including lampante (acidity 1.5%).

The extra virgin oils are generally attributed designations of controlled origin. This means that the label must truthfully indicated the geographical origin of the olives, the name of the product in accordance with the official type listing, the quantity in volume and net weight, and the name of the production or bottling plant.

• Differently from the vegetable seed oils, obtained mainly through use of solvents besides by mechanical pressing, virgin olive oil is only obtained by mechanical processes or other physical processes and must not receive any treatment other than washing, decantation, centrifugation, and filtering. The olives are harvested before they are fully ripe, when the oily substances are most concentrated, in different periods according to local climate (in Italy, for example, between November and January). Traditional, possibly manual, harvesting systems are recommended, in order to not damage the olives and to obtain highest quality oils. The fruits are then subjected to ventilation, to remove dust, twigs, and leaves, and washed under running water to eliminate all traces of soil and foreign objects.

MEDITERRANEAN
COOKING

HOW TO READ THE CARDS

DIFFICULTY	FLAVOR	NUTRITIONAL VALUE
● Easy	● Mild	● Low
●● Moderate	●● Distinctive	●● Medium
●●● Difficult	●●● Hearty, spicy	●●● High

Preparation and cooking times are shown in hours (h) and minutes (e. g. 30' is 30 minutes).

Project: Casa Editrice Bonechi
Series editor: Alberto Andreini
Coordination: Paolo Piazzesi
Graphic design and make-up: Andrea Agnorelli
Cover: Maria Rosanna Malagrinò
Editing: Rina Bucci

Translation: Paula Boomsliter

In the kitchen: Lisa Mugnai
Nutritionist: Dr. John Luke Hili

*The photographs relative to the recipes are property of the Casa Editrice Bonechi
photographic archives and were taken by* Andra Fantauzzo, Pier Silvio Ongaro, Aldo
Settembre, and Franco Tomasello.

The other photographs used in this publication are property of the Casa Editrice Bonechi
photographic archives and were taken by Luigi Di Giovine, Andrea Fantauzzo, Paolo
Giambone, M.S.A., *and* Andrea Pistolesi.
The photograph on page 148 is used with the kind permission of NET.

*For the photographs with no identified source, the Publisher would be pleased to include
the appropriate acknowledgements in any subseguent edition.*

© Copyright by CASA EDITRICE BONECHI - Florence - Italy
E-mail: bonechi@bonechi.it – Internet: www.bonechi.it

Printed in Italy by Centro Stampa Editoriale Bonechi

ISBN 88-476-0764-7

* * *

• Crushing and the later phases of processing may be performed either traditionally (olive mill) or using modern methods (hammer crusher). The mills generally use granite grindstones of variable form and size; this type of crushing does not subject the olives to excessive mechanical stress or heating, and involves less risk of pollution by metals. It is a time-consuming and expensive process involving many processing steps, but it provides greater safeguards for the quality of the oil. The so-called hammer crushing method, which entered into common use after World War II, is a rapid, continuous process that produces a smooth fine paste; it must be followed by *gramolatura* or "kneading" by special machines, which aggregates the oil present in the paste in order to favor its extraction.

• Extraction of the oil from the paste is performed according to traditional methods by hand-operated presses using piles of filter disks (once made of plant fibers, then coconut fiber, and today high-resistance synthetic fibers) on which the paste is spread. In the continuous system, the hammer crushing and *gramolatura* are followed by centrifugation, which in the main operates with the addition of water. The supporters of the traditional methods sustain that these processes both heat and "wash" the oil, thus deceasing its content of healthful substances. On the other hand, it would seem that centrifugal extraction yields an oil that while slightly more acidic is also more resistant to natural degradation.

THE MEDITERRANEAN HERBS

Basil (*Ocimum basilicum*) An annual plant native to India, widespread in the Mediterranean basin. The dark green leaves, besides being the main ingredient in pesto, are used for seasoning sauces, relishes and dressings, and salads. In folk medicine, basil is traditionally attributed antispasmodic, antiseptic, digestive, and anti-inflammatory properties.

Bay (*Laurus nobilis*) The leaves of this noble shrub, with stimulant and diuretic properties, are used in marinades and for seasoning kebabs and roasts.

Coriander (*Coriandrum sativum*) An annual herb similar to parsley. The so-called seeds (actually dried fruits) and the leaves are used in cookery. The plant possesses aperient, digestive, carminative, antispasmodic, and antiseptic properties: a true natural pharmacy!

Dill (*Anethum graveolens*) An annual herb similar to fennel, with a pungent taste and aroma, much used in Middle Eastern cooking.

Fennel (*Foeniculum vulgare*) An annual or perennial herb with a woody base: widespread in the coastal areas of the Mediterranean. The leaves are used as seasoning in sauces, dressings, and soups.

Garlic (*Allium sativum*). This aromatic bulb, native to central Asia, grows throughout the Mediterranean area and is an essential element in this region's cuisines; it is used for seasoning sauces, relishes, dressings, and soups. Its medicinal properties are well known: the ancients considered it a true cure-all – a tonic, a natural disinfectant (especially for the intestine), and an expectorant. Garlic is also used to combat hypertension, as a stimulant, and as a depurant.

Mint (*Mentha piperita*) A perennial with highly fragrant leaves which boast mild laxative, digestive, and anti-fermentative properties and are used in sauces and salads.

Oregano (*Origanum vulgare*) A hardy herb found throughout the Mediterranean area, along the coasts as well as in the highlands. The inflorescences, cut in June–August and dried, are used in sauces and for seasoning all sorts of dishes – but above all, it is an indispensable ingredient of Neapolitan pizza. The

plant possesses digestive and antiseptic properties.

Parsley (*Petroselinum crispum*) A dark green biennial herb that thrives in the shade. The aromatic leaves are used in soffritti (with garlic), marinades, and sauces. Minced or whole, a parsley garnish lends fragrance and a note of color to many dishes.

Pepper, hot red (*Capsicum annuum*) Although native to the Americas, many varieties of this plant have adapted magnificently to life in the Mediterranean area. The fruits, red and spicy-hot, are used fresh or dried to "pep up" sauces and relishes. The plant possesses digestive, antiseptic, and stimulant properties.

Sea-fennel (*Crithmum maritimum*) A perennial herb with a woody base, widespread along the Mediterranean coasts. The leaves are used in sauces, relishes, and soups.

Thyme (*Thymus vulgaris*) A small shrub with aromatic leaves, found throughout the Mediterranean area, especially near the coasts. Excellent fresh, thyme is also used dried in sauces, marinades, and salads. The plant possesses digestive and depurant properties.

A WORD FROM THE NUTRITIONIST

The phrases "Mediterranean cuisine" and "the Mediterranean diet" refer to a way of preparing foods and of eating that is common to almost all the peoples of the Mediterranean basin. In truth, such a thing does not exist, since cooking is subject to myriad national and regional interpretations; what is more, for some time now the Mediterranean has become "globalized" and has adopted eating habits common to many peoples, northern as well as southern European, and European and not.

Despite this fact, let's take a look at the dietary characteristics common to the traditions of the Mediterranean peoples. First of all, the carbohydrates: the majority (80%) are derived from the starches contained in cereals: wheat, above all, but also rice; with the addition of a few potatoes, so that what see is mainly bread and flat loaves, pasta and rice, semolina, biscuits, and all the bakery goods we know so well. These products contain sugars that are slow to be digested and assimilated by the body. The remaining carbohydrates (20%) are provided in the form of simple sugars found mainly in fruit; but the Mediterranean peoples have never said no to a fine cake prepared with beet sugar and honey.

Another salient characteristic of the Mediterranean diet regards the fats: 50% derive from extra virgin olive oil, a typical and almost exclusive product of these shores – exclusive, at least, in its time-honored production methods. Olive oil contains oleic acid, a liquid unsaturated fatty acid that contributes to preventing arteriosclerosis, as do the polyunsaturated fats found in the so-called "white" meats (poultry, rabbit, mutton) and in fish (and especially in the "blue" fishes), both of which abound in Mediterranean cooking.

The proteins derive from the meats mentioned above and less so from beef, which is richer in saturated fatty acids and used more frequently in the inland areas closer to northern Europe and the Slavic countries.

Finally, the Mediterranean diet is distinguished by its high content of both soluble and insoluble fiber, which derive from fruit and vegetables, and of vitamin C and many mineral salts. As we know, fiber prevents constipation, arteriosclerosis, high cholesterol, and many tumors.

Mediterranean eating habits, thus chemically represented, overall represent a daily calorie intake that can be attributed 60% to sugars, 25% to fats, and 15% to proteins: a healthy "pyramid" that nutritionists all over the world recommend to their patients!

THE RECIPES

ONE-DISH MEALS

VEGETABLES, SALADS, AND EGG DISHES

DESSERTS

The Tuscan Archipelago (Italy): Giglio Porto on the Isola del Giglio.

APPETIZERS AND SAUCES

1

HAMSI BOUGLAMASI

Anchovies with Lemon

800 g/1 ³/4 lbs fresh anchovies
Juice of one lemon
Parsley
Olive oil

Servings: 4	
Preparation time: 20′	
Cooking time: 10′	
Difficulty: ● ●	
Flavor: ● ●	
Kcal (per serving): 332	
Protein (per serving): 30	
Fat (per serving): 21	
Nutritional value: ● ● ●	

Clean the anchovies: cut the length of the belly from vent to head; remove entrails, head and bones. Rinse the fillets, pat dry. Arrange in layers in an fireproof serving dish with 5–6 table-spoons olive oil. Sprinkle each layer with salt, freshly-ground pepper, and chopped parsley. Drizzle with the lemon juice and olive oil. Cook covered for 8–10 minutes over medium heat, or cover with aluminum foil and bake for 15 minutes in a preheated 180°C/350°F oven. Cool before serving.

ACCIUGHE ALLE ARANCE

Anchovies with Orange

800 g/1 3/4 lbs fresh anchovies
Juice of one large orange
150 g/5–6 oz green olives
Fine dry breadcrumbs
1 hot red pepper, crushed
Pine nuts
Parsley
1 lemon
Dry white wine
Olive oil

Servings:	4
Preparation time:	15'
Cooking time:	20'
Difficulty:	● ●
Flavor:	● ●
Kcal (per serving):	726
Protein (per serving):	43
Fat (per serving):	34
Nutritional value:	● ● ●

Toast 1/3 cup breadcrumbs over low heat in a non-stick frying pan. Clean the anchovies and remove the heads, entrails, and bones. Cut the lemon into thin slices, chop the parsley, pit and chop the olives. Place a layer of anchovies in an oven-proof serving dish; arrange a few lemon slices on top and sprinkle with pine nuts, chopped parsley, olives, and hot red pepper. Continue by layers until the anchovies are used up. Salt lightly and drizzle with a few table-spoons olive oil and one cup wine. Cover with the toasted bread-crumbs. Bake in a preheated 160–180°C/300°–350°F oven for about 20 minutes, sprinkling with the orange juice after the first 10 minutes.

ARANCINI DI RISO

Rice Croquettes

Boil the rice in lightly salted water. Drain *al dente* and turn out on a working surface. Mix in the pecorino cheese, the saffron diluted in $1/2$ cup hot water, and 2 beaten eggs.

Blanch the peas; drain. Soak 2–3 tablespoons dried mushrooms in hot water; squeeze dry. Heat 2 cups or more meat sauce with the peas, the mushrooms, and a sprig of sage. Adjust the salt if required.

1 Using your hands, form a half ball of rice with a depression at the center. Fill with meat sauce mixture.

2 Add diced cheese. Form the other half of the ball, seal, and model to form a slightly pear-shaped croquette, taking care that the filling stays in the center.

3 Dredge the croquettes with flour, dip in beaten egg and roll in breadcrumbs. Fry in deep hot oil (or lard), turning frequently, until golden brown. Drain on paper towels and hold in a hot oven until ready to serve.

500 g/2 ¾ cups rice (for molds, timbales, etc.)
3 eggs
Flour
1 pinch saffron
60 g/½ cup grated pecorino cheese
120 g/¼ lb soft cheese
Fine dry breadcrumbs

Vegetable oil for frying

For the filling
Meat sauce
100 g/½ cup fresh shelled peas
Dried mushrooms
Fresh sage

Servings: 6-8	
Preparation time: 40′	
Cooking time: 2h	
Difficulty: ● ● ●	
Flavor: ● ● ●	
Kcal (per serving): 929	
Protein (per serving): 31	
Fat (per serving): 50	
Nutritional value: ● ● ●	

BRIOUATS

Sweet-and-Sour Rolls

250 g/8 oz prepared puff paste
350 g/³/4 lb ground beef
1 onion
2 eggs
Ground cinnamon, paprika, and
   ginger
Parsley
Fresh coriander leaves
Fresh chervil
Sugar
60 g/4 tbsp butter
Olive oil

Servings: 4	
Preparation time: 40′	
Cooking time: 35′	
Difficulty: ●●	
Flavor: ●●	
Kcal (per serving): 696	
Protein (per serving): 27	
Fat (per serving): 49	
Nutritional value: ●●●	

1 Mince the onion and sauté over low heat until soft, in 4 tablespoons olive oil . Do not allow to brown. Add the ground beef and cook, stirring, over low heat for about 10 minutes.

2 Add the chopped parsley, coriander and chervil, 1/4 teaspoon paprika, a pinch of ginger, 1/2 teaspoon cinnamon, and salt and pepper to taste. Stir in the beaten eggs and remove the mixture from the heat.

3 Roll out the puff paste into a thin sheet and cut into squares about 10 cm (4 inches) per side. Brush the edges with melted butter.

4 Place a tablespoon of filling on each square and roll up, taking care to seal well. Fry the rolls in deep hot oil. Drain on paper towels. Dust with cinnamon sugar and serve very hot.

CALAMARETTI AL PEPE

Squid in Pepper Sauce

500 g/1 lb *calamaretti* (young squid)
2 ripe tomatoes
1/2 medium onion
1 clove garlic
Capers
4 slices bakery bread
Peppercorns
Olive oil

Servings: 4	
Preparation time: 20′	
Cooking time: 25′	
Difficulty: ●●	
Flavor: ●●●	
Kcal (per serving): 455	
Protein (per serving): 38	
Fat (per serving): 15	
Nutritional value: ●●	

Clean the squid, removing the beaks, eyes, and all entrails. If they are very small, leave whole, otherwise detach the tentacles and cut the body crosswise into rings. Wash, seed, and dice the tomatoes. Sauté the finely-chopped onion, with the peeled garlic clove, in 3–4 tablespoons olive oil until soft

Add the squid, a dash of salt, and about 1 tablespoon peppercorns. Simmer over low heat for a few minutes, then add the tomatoes. Cover and continue cooking over very low heat for about 15 minutes.

While the squid are cooking, toast the bread slices in the oven.

Uncover the pan and raise the heat for 5 minutes to thicken the sauce. Add 1 tablespoon drained capers. Remove from heat, stir well, and let stand for five minutes.

Arrange the bread slices on a serving platter and cover with the squid in pepper sauce. Allow to cool somewhat before serving.

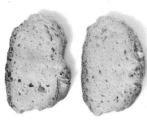

CARPACCIO DI SCAMPI

Scampi Carpaccio

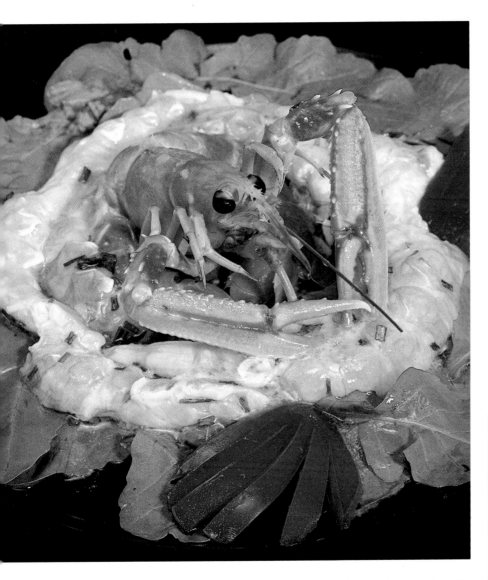

16 scampi
2 lemons
1 bunch chives
Rucola (for garnish)
2 tomatoes (for garnish)
Olive oil

Servings: 4	
Preparation time: 25' + 1h	
Difficulty: ●	
Flavor: ● ●	
Kcal (per serving): 229	
Protein (per serving): 13	
Fat (per serving): 16	
Nutritional value: ● ● ●	

Squeeze the lemons into a large bowl. Add the washed and chopped chives, 4 tablespoons of extra virgin olive oil, and a dash of salt; beat to form an emulsion. Clean the scampi and separate the tails from the heads. Reserve one or two heads for garnish. Shell the scampi and marinate in the lemon-and-oil emulsion for about 1 hour.

Make a bed of the rinsed and dried rucola on a serving platter and arrange the scampi on it. Drizzle the marinade over the top and decorate the platter with tomato slices.

CAPONATA

Trim the eggplants and cut into thin slices. Place on a rack and cover with coarse salt. Weight and let stand until the moisture is squeezed out (about one hour).

In the meantime, trim the celery and blanch for 5 minutes in slightly salted water. Drain, cut into short pieces and sauté gently in a little olive oil. Set aside.

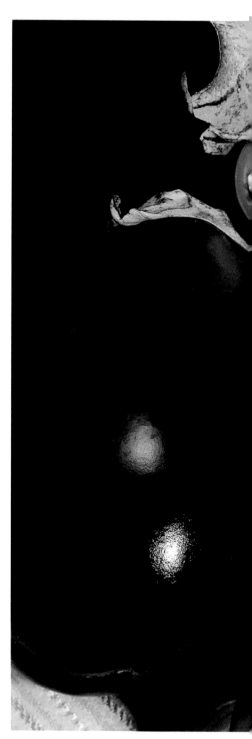

1 Skin the onions and cut into thin slices. Sauté until soft in 3–4 tablespoons olive oil together with 2 tablespoons rinsed capers, the olives, and 1/4 cup pine nuts. Trim and dice the tomatoes and add to the above ingredients. Simmer over low heat for about 20 minutes.

2 Rinse the eggplant slices and dice. Sauté in 4–5 tablespoons olive oil over high heat until they begin to brown. Add the celery and the onion and tomato mixture and mix well.

3 Cook over very low heat for about 20 minutes; add salt to taste, 1/4 teaspoon sugar and 1/3 cup vinegar. When the vinegar has evaporated remove from heat. Allow to cool before serving, garnished with a sprig of basil. The caponata will keep well for a few days in the refrigerator.

800 g/1 ³/4 lbs eggplant
3 stalks celery
2 medium onions
2–3 tomatoes
120 g/¹/4 lb pitted green olives
Fresh basil
Capers packed in salt

Pine nuts
Sugar
Wine vinegar
Coarse salt
Olive oil

Servings: 4-6	
Preparation time: 40' + 1h	
Cooking time: 1h 15'	
Difficulty: ● ● ●	
Flavor: ● ● ●	
Kcal (per serving): 389	
Protein (per serving): 9	
Fat (per serving): 29	
Nutritional value: ● ● ●	

MIDYE TAVASI BIRALI

Batter-Fried Mussels

600 g/1 1/2 lbs mussels
200 g/1 3/4 cups flour
1 cup beer
3 eggs
Vegetable oil

For the sauce
Sesame seeds
Juice of 2 lemons
3 cloves garlic
Sugar

Servings: 4	
Preparation time: 40' + 30'	
Cooking time: 25'	
Difficulty: ● ●	
Flavor: ● ●	
Kcal (per serving): 521	
Protein (per serving): 24	
Fat (per serving): 19	
Nutritional value: ● ●	

1 Prepare the batter. Mix the flour, a pinch of salt, and the beer a little at a time while stirring. Fold in the stiffly-beaten egg whites. Allow the batter to stand for 1/2 hour.

2 Scrub the mussels and remove the beards. Heat in a covered pan over low heat until opened. Shell the mussels. In a skillet, heat enough vegetable oil to float the mussels.

3 Dip the mussel meats in the batter, making sure they are uniformly coated. Fry until golden in the hot oil, turning frequently. Drain on absorbent paper. Pile in a mound on a serving platter.

4 Serve hot, with sesame sauce. In a food mixer, blend 1/3 cup sesame seeds, the peeled garlic, 1/2 teaspoon sugar and a pinch of salt. Add the lemon juice and blend again until smooth.

1

2

3

4

GAZPACHO

5-6 ripe tomatoes
2 cloves garlic
1 cucumber
1 small green pepper
5 slices bread
1 green onion
Red wine vinegar
Olive oil

Servings: 4	
Preparation time: 20' + 2h	
Difficulty: ●	
Flavor: ● ●	
Kcal (per serving): 390	
Protein (per serving): 8	
Fat (per serving): 16	
Nutritional value: ● ●	

1 Peel and dice the cucumber. Peel, seed, and dice the tomatoes; cut the onion into thin slices; remove the stem, seeds, and membranes from the pepper and chop finely. Place all these ingredients in a food mixer with the crushed garlic. Remove the crust from one slice of bread, crumble, and add. Pour in 1 tablespoon vinegar, 1 tablespoon olive oil, and salt to taste. Mix well.

2 Process at low speed to a smooth, dense consistency. Adjust the salt. Pour the gazpacho into a serving dish or stemmed bowl. Chill for about 2 hours before serving. Garnish (for example with green pepper rounds and onion rounds) and serve with the remaining bread slices, toasted.

MOSCARDINI IN INSALATA

Octopus Salad

Clean the *moscardini*, removing the beaks, eyes, and all entrails. Boil for 15 minutes in lightly salted water to which you have added 1 cup of the wine. Remove from heat and allow to cool. Drain and cut into pieces. Arrange in a serving dish and drizzle with olive oil and the lemon juice; sprinkle with the minced garlic, 2 tablespoons finely chopped parsley, and salt and pepper to taste. Chill in the warmest compartment of the refrigerator, covered, for one hour before serving.

This dish is best served cool, not cold, on a bed of lettuce and garnished with lemon and tomato wedges.

500 g/1 lb *moscardini* (*Eledone moschata*, a small octopus)
1 clove garlic
Parsley
Juice of 1 lemon
Dry white wine
Olive oil

Servings: 4
Preparation time: 20' + 1h
Cooking time: 15' + 20'
Difficulty: ●
Flavor: ● ●
Kcal (per serving): 222
Protein (per serving): 14
Fat (per serving): 11
Nutritional value: ●

SARDE MARINATE

Marinated Sardines

500 g/1 lb fresh sardines
1 carrot
1 white onion
1 stalk celery
1/2 leek
1 lemon
2–3 cloves garlic
1 bunch parsley, bay leaves
Peppercorns
Red wine vinegar
Dry white wine
Olive oil

Servings: 4	
Preparation time: 40′+ 3-4h	
Difficulty: ●	
Flavor: ● ●	
Kcal (per serving): 562	
Protein (per serving): 21	
Fat (per serving): 47	
Nutritional value: ● ● ●	

Cut the lemon in half and squeeze; grate the rind of one half. Wash and dry the parsley. Peel the carrot and onion, wash and trim the leek (white portion only) and celery and mince together. Under running water, remove the heads, entrails, and bones from the sardines; open flat like a book along the back without separating the fillets. Arrange the fish in a deep dish of adequate size (if necessary, in two layers). Sprinkle with the lemon peel, the minced vegetables, and a pinch of salt. Drizzle with a little olive oil.
Heat 2 cups vinegar and 1 cup wine in a saucepan. Pour the hot liquid over the fish and allow to cool. Add the whole garlic cloves, 1/2 tablespoon peppercorns, 2–3 bay leaves, and the minced parsley. If the liquid is insufficient to cover the fish, top up with vinegar and wine in the same proportions as above. Add the lemon juice. Allow the fish to marinate for at least 3 hours in a cool place (or in the warmest compartment of the refrigerator).
To serve, remove the fish from the marinade, drain, and arrange on a serving platter. Strain the marinade, remove the garlic cloves, and use the remaining solid ingredients as a garnish for the fish. Drizzle lightly with extra virgin olive oil just before serving.

Alternative Methods
Prepare the fish in a baking dish. Add the marinade ingredients as described above, ending with a pinch each of crushed hot red pepper and oregano. Marinate in a very slow oven (125–140°C/250–300°F) for about 1/2 hour. Drain, arrange on a serving platter, and sprinkle with more lemon juice.
Marinated sardines are also excellent fried. Remove the fish from the marinade, drain, and dry. Roll in flour and fry in hot oil (enough to float the fish) until golden. Drain on absorbent paper and sprinkle with salt before serving.

CIGALAS AL AJO

Garlic Scampi

1 Clean the scampi, remove the black dorsal vein; rinse and dry. If you are using fresh peppers, remove the stem and seeds and cut crosswise into rounds. If dried, crush and remove the seeds (Be careful not to rub your eyes afterwards! Wash your hands with soap!). Peel the garlic cloves and cut lengthwise into quarters.

2 Heat a few tablespoons olive oil in a frying pan, add the scampi, the peppers, and the garlic and sauté over high heat for 3 minutes. Add salt and pepper to taste. Serve as is or on a bed of fresh greens.

500 g/1 lb unshelled scampi
2 hot red peppers, fresh
   or dried
6–8 cloves garlic
Olive oil

Servings:	4
Preparation time:	10'
Cooking time:	5'
Difficulty:	●
Flavor:	● ●
Kcal (per serving):	283
Protein (per serving):	20
Fat (per serving):	21
Nutritional value:	●

SEPPIOLINE AI CARCIOFI

Cuttlefish with Artichokes

An excellent warm appetizer. Clean the cuttlefish (see p. 126). Wash well in running water and dry.

Trim the artichokes and remove the tough outer leaves. Blanch in the broth for 5–6 minutes; drain upside down on a cloth. When cool enough to handle, cut into wedges.

Place the artichoke wedges in a baking dish together with the cuttlefish, the finely-chopped garlic, and 3–4 tablespoons olive oil. Pour over ¹/₂ cup broth and salt and pepper to taste. Bake, covered, at 200°C/375–400°F for 15 minutes.

Remove from oven and allow to cool. Arrange the cuttlefish at the center of a serving dish, surrounded with a crown of artichoke wedges, and sprinkle with chopped parsley. Serve warm.

500 g/1 lb small cuttlefish
2 artichokes
1 clove garlic
Vegetable broth (see p. 44)
Olive oil
Parsley

Servings: 4	
Preparation time: 20' + 10'	
Cooking time: 20'	
Difficulty: ●	
Flavor: ●	
Kcal (per serving): 219	
Protein (per serving): 20	
Fat (per serving): 12	
Nutritional value: ●	

SPIEDINI DI MARE

Sea Kebabs

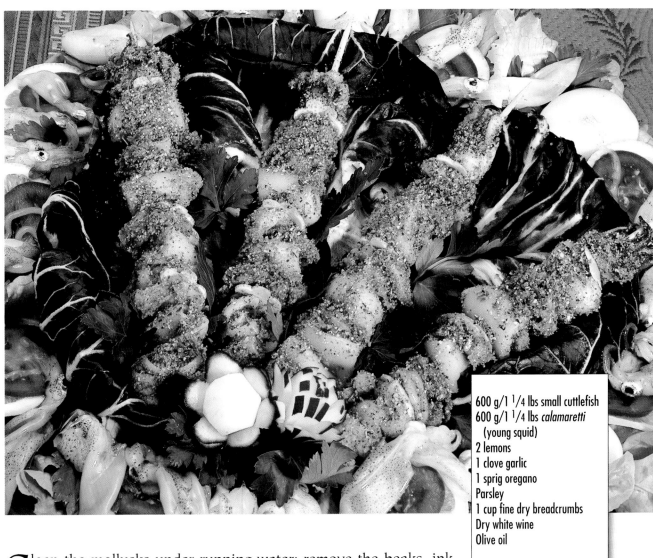

600 g/1 1/4 lbs small cuttlefish
600 g/1 1/4 lbs *calamaretti*
   (young squid)
2 lemons
1 clove garlic
1 sprig oregano
Parsley
1 cup fine dry breadcrumbs
Dry white wine
Olive oil

Servings: 4	
Preparation time: 20'	
Cooking time: 15'	
Difficulty: ●	
Flavor: ● ●	
Kcal (per serving): 395	
Protein (per serving): 42	
Fat (per serving): 15	
Nutritional value: ● ● ●	

Clean the mollusks under running water; remove the beaks, ink sacs, and all cartilaginous parts.

Toast the breadcrumbs. Mince the garlic with about 1/3 cup parsley and mix into the breadcrumbs. Add salt and pepper, a little olive oil, and 1/2 cup wine. Roll the mollusks in the breadcrumb mixture until well-coated.

Alternate cuttlefish and *calamaretti* with lemon slices on skewers. Broil on a grill or under the oven broiler, turning frequently. Use the sprig of oregano as a brush to baste the kebabs with olive oil seasoned with salt and pepper.

TOTANELLI CORSARI

Squid Buccaneer Style

500 g/1 lb *totanelli* (small squid)
2 cloves garlic
Parsley
1 hot red pepper
White wine vinegar
Olive oil

Servings: 4

Preparation time: 20'

Cooking time: 28'

Difficulty: ●

Flavor: ● ●

Kcal (per serving): 187

Protein (per serving): 18

Fat (per serving): 12

Select the smallest possible *totanelli*. Clean, wash, dry, and cut into pieces; cut the bodies into rings. Mince the garlic with about 1/3 cup parsley. Sauté over low heat, with the cut or crushed hot pepper and 4–5 tablespoons olive oil, until the garlic softens. Add the *totanelli* and a pinch of salt. Cover and cook over very low heat for about 20 minutes, stirring occasionally. Uncover the pan. Add a few drops white vinegar (or try this recipe with balsamic vinegar—excellent!), stir well and simmer uncovered for about 5 minutes to allow the sauce to thicken somewhat. Allow the *totanelli* to stand for a few minutes in their fragrant sauce before serving warm, not hot.

PESTO ALLA SICILIANA

Sicilian Pesto

Even though the traditional recipe calls for a wooden mortar and pestle, this pesto can be made with excellent results in a food mixer. Place about 2 cups basil leaves, 1/2 cup parsley, 1/4 cup pine nuts, the peeled garlic, a handful of celery leaves, and the peeled and chopped tomatoes in the mixer bowl. Blend until smooth. Transfer to a bowl and stir in 1 cup olive oil a few drops at a time. Like the better-known Ligurian pesto, the Sicilian variety is ideal as a pasta sauce, for adding a special touch to vegetable soups, and as a sauce for fried fish.

Basil
Parsley
2 or 3 tomatoes
Celery leaves
2 heads garlic
Pine nuts
Olive oil

Servings:	4
Preparation time:	20'
Difficulty:	●
Flavor:	● ● ●
Kcal (per serving):	316
Protein (per serving):	8
Fat (per serving):	27
Nutritional value:	● ● ●

AÏOLI

Aïoli Sauce

6–7 cloves garlic
3 egg yolks
1 1/2 cups olive oil

Servings: 6	
Preparation time: 20′	
Difficulty: ● ●	
Flavor: ● ● ●	
Kcal (per serving): 143	
Protein (per serving): 4	
Fat (per serving): 13	
Nutritional value: ● ● ●	

1 Have the egg yolks at room temperature. Peel the garlic, remove the sprouts, and mince. Place in a bowl and add a pinch of salt and the yolks. Stir briefly with a wooden spatula and allow to stand for 5 minutes.

2 Add the olive oil a few drops at a time while stirring with a whisk, always in the same direction. Add a pinch of pepper (if desired) and continue stirring until a mayonnaise-like consistency is reached.

Excellent with fish, meats, raw vegetables, and salads. May be prepared in a mixer.

POMMAROLA

Tomato Sauce

1 kg/2 ½ lbs ripe tomatoes
1 carrot
1 onion
1 stalk celery
1 clove garlic (optional)
1 hot red pepper (optional)
Parsley
Basil
Coarse salt
Sugar
Olive oil

Servings: 4	
Preparation time: 30′	
Cooking time: 1h 30′	
Difficulty: ●	
Flavor: ● ●	
Kcal (per serving): 180	
Protein (per serving): 4	
Fat (per serving): 11	
Nutritional value: ●	

1 Prepare the ingredients: trim and wash the vegetables and the herbs. Chop the tomatoes; slice the carrot, the onion, and the celery. Place all the vegetables in a pan with the garlic and the hot pepper (if used) over very low heat. Do not add water. Add ¼ tbsp sugar and a tablespoon or more coarse salt (to extract from the vegetables the juices in which they will cook).

2 Simmer over moderate heat (cover if necessary) for about 45 minutes. Add a few tablespoons olive oil and continue simmering for another ½ hour. Remove from heat and put through a vegetable mill, eliminating as many skins and seeds as possible. Heat again for 15 minutes. Remove from heat and add chopped parsley and basil. Allow to stand as long as possible before using; add more olive oil if desired.

SALSA ALL'ORIGANO

Oregano Sauce

2 cloves garlic
Juice of 2 lemons
Fresh oregano
Parsley
Olive oil

Servings: 4	
Preparation time: 20'	
Cooking time: 10'	
Difficulty: ●	
Flavor: ● ●	
Kcal (per serving): 144	
Protein (per serving): 1	
Fat (per serving): 15	
Nutritional value: ●	

1 Pour 1 cup olive oil into a saucepan. Beat in ½ cup hot water and the lemon juice with a fork. Add salt and pepper and one heaping tablespoon fresh oregano, about 2 tablespoons chopped parsley, and the crushed garlic.

2 Heat over (not in) hot water for 8 to 10 minutes. Pour into a heated sauce boat. This sauce is an excellent accompaniment for roast fish.
For a richer sauce, process the seeded pulp of 2–3 grilled tomatoes in a food mixer and add during the first step of the recipe.

SALSA MENTA E PREZZEMOLO

Mint and Parsley Sauce

In a food blender, chop the leaves of a large bunch of fresh mint, a handful of parsley, and the garlic. Process at low speed until reduced to a pulp.

Transfer to a bowl and add a splash of vinegar and about ³/4 cup olive oil, while stirring with a wooden spoon.

The sauce should be smooth and dense in consistency. It is perfect with grilled fish and roasted poultry and other white meats, including lamb.

Fresh mint
Parsley
2 cloves garlic
Vinegar
Olive oil

Servings:	4
Preparation time:	20'
Difficulty:	●
Flavor:	● ●
Kcal (per serving):	127
Protein (per serving):	0
Fat (per serving):	10
Nutritional value:	●

HARISSA

Harissa Sauce

250 g/¹/₂ lb hot red peppers
1 head garlic
Fresh coriander leaves
Ground dried coriander
Dried mint
Caraway seeds
Olive oil

Servings: 4

Preparation time: 20' + 1h

Difficulty: ●

Flavor: ● ● ●

Kcal (per serving): 103

Protein (per serving): 1

Fat (per serving): 10

Nutritional value: ●

1 Remove the stems and seeds from the peppers and allow to stand in water to cover for about one hour.

2 Drain the peppers. In a food blender, chop with 3 tablespoons fresh coriander leaves, the garlic, and one tablespoon each of the other spices. Transfer to a bowl and mix in a few teaspoons olive oil. The finished sauce should be very dense.
It can be kept refrigerated in a glass jar with hermetic seal. Every time you use the *harissa*, add enough oil to the jar to cover the surface of the sauce, in order to avoid off-flavors and the formation of mold.

Harissa sauce is an omnipresent condiment on the tables of the Maghreb and the Middle East. It lends a spicy touch to couscous, soups and stews, roast meats, and vegetable dishes. Although tradition calls for a mortar and pestle, the blender version given above is also excellent – or buy it ready-to-use!

SOUPS, PASTA, AND RICE

2

BOUILLABAISSE

This tasty fish stew from Provence is reminiscent of the Italian cacciucco *but is actually quite different (just think of the saffron and the lobster). Frozen lobster is a fine (and much less expensive) substitute for fresh.*

1 Clean and rinse all the fish and cut into pieces. Break the lobster in half lengthwise.

2 Mince the leek and onion and sauté in 5–6 tablespoons olive oil. Add the garlic and the tomato purée and simmer over low heat.

3 Add all the fish and about 2 cups of hot water. Salt and pepper to taste; stir well.

4 Add the saffron, minced parsley, and a few tablespoons olive oil and cook over medium heat for 30 minutes. Toast the bread; place in the bottoms of individual serving dishes and cover with the bouillabaisse.

800 g/1 ³/4 lbs assorted stewing fish (mullet, whitefish, halibut, scorpion-fish or gurnard, angler fish, mackerel, sea bass or weaver, etc.)
4–5 red rock mullets
1 small lobster
1 small cod, hake, or hound fish (200 g/¹/2 lb)
1 leek
1 green onion
1–2 cloves garlic
300 g/1 ¹/4 cups tomato purée
Parsley
1–2 envelopes saffron
6 slices bakery bread
Olive oil

Servings: 6	
Preparation time: 30′	
Cooking time: 40′	
Difficulty: ● ● ●	
Flavor: ●	
Kcal (per serving): 597	
Protein (per serving): 45	
Fat (per serving): 27	
Nutritional value: ● ●	

1

2

PASTITSIO

Pasta au Gratin

600 g/1 ¹/₂ lbs ground beef
1 onion
400 g/1 ³/₄ cups crushed
   tomatoes
1 bunch parsley
150 g/5–6 oz Parmesan or
   Greek *kefalotiri* cheese, grated
500 g/1 lb ziti pasta
70 g/5 tbsp butter
50 g/5–6 tbsp flour
Milk
White wine
Ground nutmeg
Ground cinnamon
Ground hot red pepper
3 eggs
Olive oil

Servings: 6	
Preparation time: 30'	
Cooking time: 2h	
Difficulty: ●●	
Flavor: ●●●	
Kcal (per serving): 1196	
Protein (per serving): 44	
Fat (per serving): 38	
Nutritional value: ●●●	

1 Dice the onion and sauté lightly in 4 tablespoons olive oil. Add the ground beef and sauté until slightly browned. Add the tomatoes, the minced parsley, a pinch of cinnamon and a pinch of red pepper, 1 cup white wine, salt and pepper. Simmer over low heat for about 30 minutes.

2 While the meat sauce is cooking, prepare the bechamel sauce. Melt the butter in a saucepan, reserving 1 ¹/₂ tablespoons. Stir in the flour. When the roux begins brown, pour in 1 ¹/₄ cups cold milk.

3 Begin stirring at once and cook the sauce over low heat for 12–15 minutes, stirring constantly. When the bechamel has thickened, add salt and pepper to taste and a pinch of nutmeg. Remove from the heat.

4 When the bechamel has cooled, stir in two beaten eggs. Stir the other egg into the cooled meat sauce. Cook the pasta and drain *al dente*. Place half the quantity in the bottom of a buttered oven-proof serving dish. Sprinkle with half the cheese and cover with the meat sauce. Make another layer with the rest of the pasta, pour over the bechamel and sprinkle with the rest of the cheese. Bake in as 180°C/350°F oven for 40–45 minutes.

FUSILLI GAMBERETTI E OLIVE

Pasta with Shrimp and Olives

400 g/14 oz *fusilli* pasta
150 – 200/¹/₃ – ¹/₂ lb
  precooked shrimp
1 clove garlic
1 onion
300 g/1 ¹/₄ cups crushed
  tomatoes
60 g/2 oz pitted black olives
50 g/2 tbsp capers in vinegar,
  drained
Fresh basil leaves
Parsley
Olive oil

Servings: 4	
Preparation time: 10' + 2h	
Cooking time: 20'	
Difficulty: ●	
Flavor: ● ● ●	
Kcal (per serving): 523	
Protein (per serving): 20	
Fat (per serving): 12	
Nutritional value: ● ●	

1 Cut the onion into paper-thin slices, chop the garlic, and sauté until soft in 4 tablespoons olive oil. Add the tomatoes and salt and pepper to taste; simmer for about 10 minutes. Add a handful of basil leaves and cook for another 2–3 minutes. Remove from heat and allow to cool.

2 Transfer the sauce to a glass or terracotta container. Add the shrimp and the chopped capers and olives. Cover with plastic wrap and refrigerate for at least two hours. While the pasta is cooking, reheat the sauce and sprinkle with minced parsley. Drain the pasta, toss with the sauce, and serve at once.

LAGANE E FAGIOLI

Pasta and Beans

1 Make a well with the flour, add a pinch of salt and all the luke-warm water needed to form a smooth dough. Form into a ball and allow to stand for about 1 hour. Meanwhile, cook the fresh beans in salted water (about 1 hour). Roll out the pasta dough and cut into broad strips (*lagane*).

2 Cook the pasta *al dente*. A few minutes before draining, melt the lard, add the whole red peppers and the peeled garlic, and simmer over very low heat for a few minutes. Drain the pasta and mix with the drained beans. Remove the peppers and garlic from the lard; pour over the pasta and toss.

500 g/4 cups white flour + 50 g/4 tbsp for the working surface
500 g/1 lb shelled fresh borlotti or pinto beans
3 fresh hot red peppers
2 cloves garlic
250 g/¹/₂ lb lard

Servings:	6
Preparation time:	30' + 1h
Cooking time:	1h 15'
Difficulty:	●●
Flavor:	●●
Kcal (per serving):	828
Protein (per serving):	17
Fat (per serving):	44
Nutritional value:	●●●

PASTA CON ACCIUGA E PANGRATTATO

Pasta with Anchovies and Breadcrumbs

350 g/12 oz linguini or *reginette* pasta
250 g/¹/₂ lb wild fennel tips (cymes)
5 salt-cured anchovies
1 clove garlic
¹/₄ cup pine nuts
¹/₄ cup white raisins
Parsley
Hot red pepper
Fine dry breadcrumbs
Olive oil

Servings: 4	
Preparation time: 30′	
Cooking time: 20′	
Difficulty: ● ●	
Flavor: ● ● ●	
Kcal (per serving): 740	
Protein (per serving): 25	
Fat (per serving): 30	
Nutritional value: ● ● ●	

1 Wash and remove the heads and bones from the anchovies. Soak the raisins in warm water. Sauté a sprig of parsley and the crushed garlic in 3–4 tablespoons olive oil until the garlic is just golden. Remove both from the pan and crush the anchovy fillets into the oil with a fork. Add the pine nuts and the drained and squeezed raisins.

2 Transfer the sauce to a bowl. Add a few teaspoons olive oil to the pan and toast about ¹/₂ cup breadcrumbs over high heat. Blanch the fennel tips in boiling salted water; remove, and use the same water to cook the pasta. Drain al dente and toss with the sauce, the toasted breadcrumbs, and a pinch of crushed hot red pepper.

You may substitute grouper or gurnard for the cuoccio, or scorpion fish, with excellent results

LINGUINE AL "CUOCCIO"

Linguini "al Cuoccio"

Place the fish in a deep pan with the tomatoes cut in half lengthwise, the minced parsley, the garlic, the olive oil, and a sprinkling of crushed hot pepper. Cover with aluminum foil and simmer over very low heat until the fish is cooked through.

Add salt to taste to the sauce. Remove the fish; bone and clean; cut the meat into small pieces. Hold over hot water with a little of the sauce until ready to use.

While the linguini are cooking in boiling salted water, continue simmering the sauce, uncovered, until it thickens. Drain the pasta while still very *al dente* and turn out into the pan of simmering sauce.

Mix well, add a few sprigs of basil, and transfer to a serving dish. Right before serving, top with the pieces of fish in the reserved sauce.

350 g/12 oz linguini pasta
1 scorpion fish,
    about 1 kg/2 1/2 lbs
500 g/1 lb peeled tomatoes
2 cloves garlic
Parsley, Basil
1 hot red pepper
Olive oil

Servings: 4	
Preparation time: 25'	
Cooking time: 45'	
Difficulty: ● ●	
Flavor: ● ● ●	
Kcal (per serving): 602	
Protein (per serving): 47	
Fat (per serving): 13	
Nutritional value: ● ● ●	

HARIRA

Harira Soup

1 Soak the lentils in cold water for about one hour; simmer for about one hour with the onion. Drain and return to the pan with the vegetable broth, 1/2 teaspoon saffron and a pinch of pepper. Stew over low heat for 1/2 hour.

2 While the lentils are cooking, prepare the *tedouirà* sauce. Place the coriander, 1 tablespoon minced parsley, the chopped tomatoes, the lemon juice, the butter, a pinch of salt, and one quart water in a deep pan.

3 Cook the sauce over high heat for 1/2 hour. Blend in the flour and add the drained lentils. Serve the *harira* soup hot.

Prepare the vegetable broth by simmering a carrot, an onion, a stalk of celery, and a small tomato for 1/2 hour in lightly salted water – or use a vegetable bouillon cube.

220 g/¹/₂ lb lentils
Vegetable broth (see facing page)
Powdered saffron

For the tedouirà sauce
4 ripe tomatoes
1 onion
Juice of 1 lemon

2 tbsp flour
1 tbsp ground coriander
Parsley
30 g/2 tbsp butter

Servings: 4	
Preparation time: 20′ + 1h	
Cooking time: 1h 30′	
Difficulty: ● ●	
Flavor: ● ●	
Kcal (per serving): 313	
Protein (per serving): 15	
Fat (per serving): 8	
Nutritional value: ● ●	

PASTICCIO DI CARNI IN CROSTA

Meat Pie

1 young hen,
   1.2 kg/ca. 2 1/2 lbs
1 onion
4–5 ripe tomatoes
10 chicken livers
10 veal sweetbreads
1 sausage
Cinnamon
2 hard-boiled eggs, sliced
1 egg yolk
Olive oil

For the pastry
300 g/2 1/2 cups flour
150 g/3/4 cup butter

Servings: 6	
Preparation time: 1h + 1h	
Cooking time: 1h	
Difficulty: ●●●	
Flavor: ●●●	
Kcal (per serving): 1293	
Protein (per serving): 46	
Fat (per serving): 61	
Nutritional value: ●●●	

1 Blend the softened butter with the flour and a pinch of salt. Roll out the pastry, fold into thirds, and allow to stand for 1/2 hour. Roll out and fold again; allow to stand for 1/2 hour.

2 Sauté the sliced onion in 4–5 tablespoons olive oil until transparent. Flame, rinse, dry, and cut up the hen; blanch the sweetbreads. Add to

the onions and sauté for 10 minutes. Add the diced tomatoes and the cleaned livers and cook for 10 minutes longer.

3 Remove the pieces of hen and the livers. Bone the hen and chop the livers coarsely; return to the pan. Add the crumbled sausage and a pinch of cinnamon. Sauté over high heat for about 10 minutes.

4 Roll out the pastry into two unequal sheets. With the larger, line a greased oven-proof pan; pour in the meat mixture. Cover with slices of boiled egg. Cover with the second sheet of pasta. Fold over and seal the edges; pierce the top with a fork. Bake at 180°C/350°F for 30 minutes.
Beat the egg yolk with a little water and brush over the upper crust a few minutes before the end of the baking time.

For the soup
1 onion
1 leek
2 ripe tomatoes
4 potatoes
200 g/¹/₂ lb green beans
40 g/3 tbsp butter
Vegetable broth (see p. 44)

For the pistou
5–6 cloves garlic
150 g/5–6 oz basil leaves
4 ripe tomatoes (optional)
100 g/¹/₄ lb Parmesan cheese,
   grated
2 tbsp pine nuts (optional)
Extra virgin olive oil

Servings: 4	
Preparation time: 25' + 15'	
Cooking time: 50'	
Difficulty: ● ●	
Flavor: ● ● ●	
Kcal (per serving): 447	
Protein (per serving): 12	
Fat (per serving): 23	
Nutritional value: ● ●	

SOUPE AU PISTOU

Vegetable Soup with Pistou

Rinse and trim the tomatoes and the green beans; peel the potatoes. Rinse the leek thoroughly to remove any soil between the layers. Cut off the tops of the leaves. Peel the onion. Cut the leek and the onion into paper-thin slices and sauté in the melted butter until soft. Add the diced tomatoes and potatoes and the green beans cut into short sections. Salt and pepper to taste. Add 2 cups vegetable broth and simmer over very low heat for about 45 minutes, adding more hot broth if necessary.
Serve the soup hot with the pistou and extra virgin olive oil on the side.

To prepare the pistou, first rinse a large bunch of basil under cold running water and dry between two kitchen towels. Separate the leaves from the stems. Place the basil leaves, the peeled garlic, and the peeled and seeded tomatoes and the pine nuts (if used) in a food mixer and chop at low speed to a rather coarse consistency. Add the cheese (you may use pecorino instead of Parmesan, but be sure it is neither too salty nor too hard) and blend for a few seconds at medium speed. Transfer the pistou to a bowl and add extra virgin olive oil a little at a time, while mixing, until the sauce is fluid but not runny. Allow to stand before using.
Pistou keeps well for 2–3 weeks covered with a film of oil in hermetically-sealed glass jars.
Store in a dark place.

ORECCHIETTE CON I BROCCOLI

Orecchiette* with Broccoli

Blanch the broccoli in boiling water for 5 minutes. Drain and keep warm. Reserve the water used for blanching.

While the pasta is cooking in boiling salted water, heat a few tablespoons olive oil in a small pan; add the minced garlic, the hot pepper, and the anchovy fillets. Cook over low heat for 3–4 minutes, adding a few tablespoons of the broccoli water. Drain the *orecchiette* and return to the pan; add the broccoli, the anchovy sauce, a dash of black pepper.

Serve as is or with a sprinkling of pecorino or Parmesan cheese.

* A specialty pasta of Puglia (Italy), which as the name indicates resembles small ears or caps.

400 g/14 oz *orecchiette* pasta
200 g/¹/₂ lb broccoli florets
2 cloves garlic
1 hot red pepper
2 anchovy fillets packed in oil
Olive oil

Servings: 4	
Preparation time: 10′	
Cooking time: 20′	
Difficulty: ●	
Flavor: ● ●	
Kcal (per serving): 502	
Protein (per serving): 17	
Fat (per serving): 13	
Nutritional value: ● ●	

PASTICCIO DI PASTA

Macaroni Pie

400 g/14 oz fluted macaroni	2 hard-boiled eggs	Servings: 6	
100 g/¹/4 lb ground beef	1 mozzarella	Preparation time: 30' + 1h	
10 chicken livers	Grated *caciocavallo* cheese	Cooking time: 1h 10'	
50 g/¹/8 lb salami	Basil	Difficulty: ● ● ●	
5–6 ripe tomatoes, peeled	Olive oil	Flavor: ● ● ●	
100 g/¹/4 lb shelled fresh peas		Kcal (per serving): 826	
1 onion		Protein (per serving): 44	
1 eggplant		Fat (per serving): 32	
1 clove garlic		Nutritional value: ● ● ●	

1 Slice the eggplant, sprinkle the slices with salt and allow to stand, weighted, for ¹/2 hour until the moisture is squeezed out.
Rinse, dry, and sauté until golden in 4–5 tablespoons olive oil.

2 In another pan, sauté the onions, sliced lengthwise, and the crushed garlic in 4–5 tablespoons olive oil until soft. Add the ground beef and livers and sauté until lightly browned; add the peas. Salt and pepper to taste. Add the chopped tomatoes and simmer over low heat for ¹/2 hour. Remove the garlic clove.

The smoking cone of Sicily's Mount Etna.

3 Cook the pasta. Drain while still very *al dente* and toss with the sauce, the mozzarella cut into thin strips, the grated cheese, the sliced eggs, the chopped salami, and a few basil leaves. Lay the eggplant slices in the bottom of an oven-proof dish; cover with the pasta mixture. Bake at 180°C/350°F for 15 minutes. Turn out on a platter and garnish as desired.

RISO ALLE MELANZANE

Rice with Eggplant

350 g/1 3/4 cups rice
2–3 eggplants
4–5 ripe tomatoes
1 onion
Basil, parsley, saffron
Hard pecorino cheese with
   peppercorns, grated
Olive oil

Servings: 6	
Preparation time: 20' + 1h	
Cooking time: 40'	
Difficulty: ● ●	
Flavor: ● ● ●	
Kcal (per serving): 585	
Protein (per serving): 24	
Fat (per serving): 18	
Nutritional value: ● ●	

Slice the eggplant, sprinkle the slices with salt and allow to stand, weighted, until the moisture is squeezed out.
Rinse, dry, and sauté until golden in 3–4 tablespoons olive oil.
Sauté the sliced onion until soft in 4–5 tablespoons olive oil with a generous amount of minced basil and parsley. Add the chopped tomatoes, salt, and pepper, and simmer over low heat for 15 minutes. Boil the rice in slightly salted water to which you have added an envelope of saffron. Drain *al dente*. Place a layer of rice in the bottom of an oven-proof dish; cover with tomato-eggplant sauce. Repeat this operation until the ingredients are used up, ending with a layer of sauce.
Dust with grated cheese and bake in a hot 200°C/375–400°F oven for about 10 minutes. Sprinkle with minced parsley and basil before serving.

RISOTTO DEI CICLOPI

Seafood Risotto

Scrub and de-beard the mussels; open them in a pan with a few tablespoons olive oil. Remove the meats from the shells and reserve the cooking liquid. Mince the garlic with parsley; heat in a frying pan with 4 tablespoons olive oil. Add the cleaned and coarsely chopped squid and shrimp, and the filleted anchovy. Simmer for 4–5 minutes. Add the chopped tomatoes and about 1/4 cup strained mussel liquor. Simmer over low heat for about 15 minutes. Add the rice and cook, stirring occasionally and adding hot mussel liquor as needed. Add the shelled mussels about 5 minutes before the rice is completely cooked. Serve immediately.

300 g/1 2/3 cups rice
200 g/1/2 lb *calamaretti*
   (young squid)
400 g/1 lb mussels
120 g/1/4 lb small shrimp
1 anchovy
3–4 ripe tomatoes
1 clove garlic
Parsley
Olive oil

Servings: 4	
Preparation time: 20'	
Cooking time: 40'	
Difficulty: ● ●	
Flavor: ● ●	
Kcal (per serving): 488	
Protein (per serving): 23	
Fat (per serving): 13	
Nutritional value: ● ●	

TIMBALLO DI RISO

Rice Timbale

400 g/2 1/4 cups "Vialone" rice
80 g/3 oz pork rinds (optional)
1 sausage
100 g/1/4 lb Sicilian *toma* (or
   other low-fat cow's milk cheese)
100 g/1/4 lb provola cheese
1 onion
Tomato paste
Parsley
Fine dry breadcrumbs
Lard (or butter)
Olive oil

For the broth
1 boiling hen, 1 kg/ca. 2 1/2 lbs
1 carrot
1 onion
1 stalk celery
2–3 cherry tomatoes

For the meat balls
180 g/6-8 oz ground beef
Hard pecorino cheese with
   peppercorns, grated
2 eggs
1 clove garlic
Parsley
1 slice bread with the crusts
   removed, soaked in milk

Servings: 6	
Preparation time: 25' + 1h	
Cooking time: 50'	
Difficulty: ● ● ●	
Flavor: ● ●	
Kcal (per serving): 1455	
Protein (per serving): 55	
Fat (per serving): 83	
Nutritional value: ● ● ●	

1 With a fork, mix together the ground beef, the eggs, the minced garlic and parsley, the soaked bread (from which you have squeezed out the excess liquid), and salt and pepper to taste. Form the mixture into small balls. Boil the hen with the carrot, celery, onion, the tomatoes, and half of the meat balls.

2 Slice the other onion and sauté until soft in about 1 tablespoon lard (or butter). Add the crumbled sausage and the diced pork rinds and sauté until lightly browned. Add chopped parsley, 1 tablespoon tomato paste diluted with water, and the remaining meat balls. Cover and cook over low heat for about 25 minutes.

3 Bone the hen; chop the meat coarsely and keep warm with the boiled meat balls. Cook the rice in the broth. Drain *al dente*; transfer to a bowl and mix in ½ cup or more grated pecorino cheese.

4 In a greased oven-proof dish dusted with bread crumbs, place a layer of rice, hen, and boiled meat-balls, and top with the sliced toma cheese. Cover with a layer of meatballs in sauce, sausage, and pork rinds, and top with the diced provola cheese. Cover with the rest of the rice mixed with the remaining hen. Sprinkle with more grated pecorino cheese and salt and pepper. Bake in a hot 200°C/375–400°F oven for about 10 minutes.

SEDANI A "PICCHI-PACCHI"

"Picchi-Pacchi" Macaroni

1 Cut the onion into thin lengthwise strips. Sauté over low heat in 3–4 tablespoons olive oil until soft, with the crushed garlic and a sprig of basil. Add the rinsed and chopped tomatoes. Cook over high heat until thickened; add salt and pepper to taste.

2 Slice the eggplant and sauté the slices in 3–4 tablespoons olive oil until golden. Rinse and bone the anchovies. Add both these ingredients to the tomato sauce and break up with a fork.
Cook and drain the pasta and toss with the sauce.

350 g/12 oz *penne* or *sedani* macaroni
4 ripe tomatoes
1 onion
1 eggplant
1 clove garlic
2–3 salted anchovies
Basil
Olive oil

Servings: 4	
Preparation time: 30'	
Cooking time: 40'	
Difficulty: ●●	
Flavor: ●●●	
Kcal (per serving): 506	
Protein (per serving): 17	
Fat (per serving): 18	
Nutritional value: ●●	

SEDANI AL GRATIN

Macaroni au Gratin

Brown the meat with the sliced onions in 3–4 tablespoons olive oil. Pour over about 1 cup red wine. Add salt, the clove, a pinch of cinnamon, and a bay leaf; cover and simmer over low heat for about one hour or until the meat is tender.

Draw off about 1 cup of the meat liquor and mix with $1/2$ of the ricotta cheese. Adjust salt and pepper.

Boil the pasta and drain when about 4/5 cooked. Place the pasta in a greased oven-proof dish; toss with the ricotta mixture and about $1/2$ cup of grated pecorino cheese.

Dot the top of the casserole with the remaining ricotta cheese and sprinkle with grated pecorino and a pinch of cinnamon. Brown in a hot 200°C/375–400°F oven for about 10 minutes.

Serve the beef as your main course.

350 g/12 oz fluted *sedani* macaroni
250 g/$1/2$ lb fresh sheep's milk ricotta cheese
Grated pecorino cheese
Ground cinnamon
Olive oil

For the roast
350 g/$3/4$ lb beef (round, chuck, etc.)
1 onion, 1 clove
Bay leaf, cinnamon
Red wine

Servings: 4	
Preparation time: 40'	
Cooking time: 1h 30'	
Difficulty: ● ●	
Flavor: ● ● ●	
Kcal (per serving): 751	
Protein (per serving): 30	
Fat (per serving): 28	
Nutritional value: ● ● ●	

350 g/12 oz fluted *sedani* macaroni
4-5 ripe tomatoes
2 sweet peppers
1 clove garlic
Parsley
Hot red pepper
Grated pecorino cheese
Olive oil

Servings: 4	
Preparation time: 20′	
Cooking time: 30′	
Difficulty: ●●	
Flavor: ●●●	
Kcal (per serving): 506	
Protein (per serving): 16	
Fat (per serving): 17	
Nutritional value: ●●	

SEDANI AL PEPERONE

Macaroni with Peppers

Wash the peppers and cut in half lengthwise. Remove the stems, seeds, and white fibrous membranes. Broil 3 pepper halves and reserve the fourth raw. Clean and dice the tomatoes.
Sauté the garlic until just golden in 3–4 tablespoons olive oil. Add 1–2 tablespoons chopped parsley, the tomatoes, and $1/2$ crushed hot red pepper. Cut the broiled peppers into chunks and add to the sauce. Simmer until thickened (15 minutes).
Boil the pasta, drain *al dente*, and add to the sauce. Toss briefly. Sprinkle with grated pecorino cheese and garnish with the diced raw sweet pepper.

58

SEDANI SARDE E PISELLI

Macaroni with Sardines and Peas

Clean the sardines and remove the heads, bones and tails. Sauté the sliced onion in 3–4 tablespoons olive oil with the peas and a sprig of parsley, while stirring, until the onion is soft. After 5–6 minutes add the sardines and salt and pepper to taste.

Boil the pasta; drain *al dente* and add to the sauce. Toss briefly in the pan. Serve immediately.

350 g/12 oz fluted "sedani" macaroni
1/2 onion
Parsley
300 g/3/4 lb fresh sardines
150 g/3/4 cup shelled peas
Olive oil

Servings: 4
Preparation time: 15'
Cooking time: 20'
Difficulty: ● ●
Flavor: ● ●
Kcal (per serving): 276
Protein (per serving): 10
Fat (per serving): 21
Nutritional value: ● ●

350 g/12 oz spaghetti (or thin
   spaghetti)
4-5 ripe tomatoes
Basil
2 cloves garlic
Hot red pepper
Salted hard ricotta (or pecorino)
   cheese, for grating
Olive oil

Servings: 4	
Preparation time: 15' + 1h	
Cooking time: 8'	
Difficulty: ●	
Flavor: ● ●	
Kcal (per serving): 507	
Protein (per serving): 18	
Fat (per serving): 18	
Nutritional value: ● ●	

SPAGHETTI ALLA CARRETTIERA

Spaghetti with Tomatoes and Ricotta

Wash and trim the tomatoes; dice into a bowl with the garlic minced with at least 2 handfuls of basil leaves. Add olive oil, salt, and the red pepper; mix well and allow to stand for about 1 hour.
Boil the pasta and drain *al dente*. Toss with the sauce and sprinkle lavishly with grated cheese. Serve immediately.

SPAGHETTI ALLA MARINARA

Spaghetti Fisherman Style

Wash, trim, and dice the tomatoes. Rinse and clean the fish; cut into chunks. Sauté the sliced onion in 3–4 tablespoons olive oil with a sprig of parsley. Add the tomatoes and simmer for about 10 minutes.

Add the fish and enough water to cover; salt and pepper to taste. Cook over high heat until the water has evaporated and the sauce thickened. Remove the fish and keep it warm.

Boil the spaghetti and drain *al dente*. Toss with the sauce. Serve the fish as your main course.

300 g/10-12 oz spaghetti (or thin spaghetti)
700 g/1 $^1/_2$ lbs assorted small fish (sea bass or perch, dentex, etc.)
4-5 ripe tomatoes
1 onion
Parsley
Olive oil

Servings:	4
Preparation time:	30'
Cooking time:	20'
Difficulty:	● ●
Flavor:	● ● ●
Kcal (per serving):	575
Protein (per serving):	42
Fat (per serving):	18
Nutritional value:	● ●

SPAGHETTI ALLE MELANZANE

Spaghetti with Eggplant

12 oz spaghetti
2 small eggplants (or 1 large)
4-5 ripe tomatoes
1 onion
Basil
Grated Parmesan cheese
Olive oil

Servings: 4	
Preparation time: 25' + 30'	
Cooking time: 50'	
Difficulty: ● ●	
Flavor: ● ●	
Kcal (per serving): 497	
Protein (per serving): 16	
Fat (per serving): 14	
Nutritional value: ● ●	

Slice the eggplant, sprinkle the slices with salt and allow to stand, weighted, for $1/2$ hour until the moisture is squeezed out.

Rinse, dry, and dice the slices. Sauté until golden in about 4 tablespoons olive oil; set aside.

Sauté the sliced onion in 4–5 tablespoons olive oil until soft; add the diced tomatoes, a sprig of basil, and salt and pepper to taste. Cook over low heat for about $1/2$ hour, then blend the sauce in a food mixer.

Boil the spaghetti and drain while still very *al dente*. Toss with the sauce; sauté briefly with the eggplant. Serve sprinkled with Parmesan cheese and garnished with sprigs of basil.

SPAGHETTI ALLE ZUCCHINE

Spaghetti with Zucchini

350 g/12 oz thin spaghetti
3-4 zucchini
1 clove garlic
100 g/¹/4 lb pecorino cheese
   with peppercorns or salted
   hard ricotta cheese, for grating
Olive oil

Servings:	4
Preparation time:	10′
Cooking time:	15′
Difficulty:	●
Flavor:	●●
Kcal (per serving):	850
Protein (per serving):	46
Fat (per serving):	35
Nutritional value:	●●●

Trim the zucchini and cut into thin rounds. Sauté the crushed garlic until golden in 4–5 tablespoons olive oil. Remove the garlic and sauté the zucchini rounds until golden over high heat in the flavored olive oil. Add salt and pepper; set aside and keep warm.
Boil the spaghetti and drain *al dente*. Sprinkle with the grated cheese, mix, and toss with the zucchini and their oil.
Serve immediately. Simple – and delicious!

SPAGHETTI IN ERBA

Spaghetti with Herbs

500 g/1 lb spaghetti
1 bouquet garni (rosemary,
  parsley, thyme, 4-5 bay
  leaves, 4-5 leaves sage)
4 tbsp minced herbs: rosemary,
  basil, and thyme
6 cloves garlic
1 hot red pepper
800 g/1 lb 12 oz chopped,
  seeded tomatoes (3 1/2 cups)
1 tsp red wine vinegar
Olive oil

Servings: 6	
Preparation time: 10'	
Cooking time: 30'	
Difficulty: ●	
Flavor: ●●●	
Kcal (per serving): 485	
Protein (per serving): 13	
Fat (per serving): 11	
Nutritional value: ●●	

1 Place the peeled and minced garlic and the hot pepper in a large frying pan (use later to toss the pasta) with 6 tablespoons olive oil.

2 Add a pinch of salt; cook the garlic for 2–3 minutes over moderate heat. Add the tomatoes, the bouquet garni, and salt if necessary. Mix well; cover halfway and simmer for 15 minutes. When the sauce begins to thicken, remove from the heat and discard the bouquet garni. Boil the spaghetti and drain while still very *al dente*. Add to the sauce in the pan, add the vinegar, cover and heat for about 2 minutes. Sprinkle with half the minced herbs and mix well. Serve in heated bowls, sprinkled with the remaining minced herbs.

SPAGHETTINI AL NERO

Black Spaghetti

350 g/12 oz thin spaghetti
350 g/³/4 lb cuttlefish (with ink sacs)
1 onion
300 g/12 oz peeled tomatoes (1 ¹/2 cups)
Parsley
Hard pecorino cheese
Olive oil

Servings:	4
Preparation time:	15'
Cooking time:	25'
Difficulty:	● ●
Flavor:	● ●
Kcal (per serving):	567
Protein (per serving):	30
Fat (per serving):	19
Nutritional value:	● ●

Clean the cuttlefish and remove the bone, being careful not to pierce the ink sacs. Reserve. Cut the meat into strips. Sauté the sliced onion until transparent in 4–5 tablespoons olive oil, with about 1 tablespoon chopped parsley.
Add the cuttlefish and the tomatoes; cover and simmer for about 20 minutes. Uncover, add 2–3 ink sacs, and simmer until thickened.
Boil the spaghetti and drain while still very *al dente*. Toss briefly with the sauce over low heat. Sprinkle with grated pecorino cheese and serve at once.

VERMICELLINI VERACI

Spaghetti with Clams

350 g/12 oz *vermicellini* (very thin spaghetti)
1 kg/2 ¹/4 lbs small hard-shell clams (*vongole veraci*)
1 clove garlic
4–5 ripe tomatoes
Dry white wine
Parsley
Olive oil

Servings: 4	
Preparation time: 30′	
Cooking time: 45′	
Difficulty: ● ●	
Flavor: ● ●	
Kcal (per serving): 442	
Protein (per serving): 12	
Fat (per serving): 12	
Nutritional value: ● ●	

Rinse the tomatoes; cut in half and remove the seeds. Scrub and soak the clams; place in a large frying pan with a few tablespoons olive oil and ¹/2 cup wine. Cover and cook over high heat until the clams open. Remove from the heat: strain the cooking liquor. Keep warm. In another pan, sauté the crushed garlic in 4–5 tablespoons olive oil until it just begins to color; remove from the oil. Add the diced tomatoes, about 1 cup of the clam liquor, and salt and pepper to taste. Cook for about 10 minutes.

While the sauce is cooking, boil the pasta and drain when ⁴/5 cooked (5–6 minutes cooking time).

Add the clams to the sauce. Transfer the pasta to the pan containing the clam sauce; toss until well coated and hold over low heat until cooked *al dente*.

Serve immediately sprinkled with minced parsley. Cheese? No thanks!!

SOPA DE AJO

Garlic Soup

300 g/3/4 lb day-old bread
1 head garlic
Ground hot red pepper
1 liter/4 cups beef broth
Olive oil

Servings:	4
Preparation time:	10'
Cooking time:	35'
Difficulty:	●
Flavor:	● ● ●
Kcal (per serving):	360
Protein (per serving):	8
Fat (per serving):	11
Nutritional value:	● ●

Cut the bread into cubes; peel the garlic cloves and chop coarse-ly. Heat a few tablespoons olive oil in a deep frying pan and toast the bread cubes over low heat. Add the garlic, 1/4–1/2 tea-spoon ground red pepper, and 1 liter broth. Add salt if desired. Cook, covered, for about 20 minutes over low heat.

Heat the oven to 200°C/375–400°F. Divide the bread mixture into four portions in individual oven-proof serving dishes. Brown on the center rack for 10 minutes.

Serve straight from the oven. For a richer dish, try breaking an egg into a well at the center of each dish or sprinkling with Swiss or Parmesan cheese before baking.

M'DESHESHA

Tomato Soup

300 g/1 ¹/4 cups tomato purée
5 cloves garlic
100 g/¹/4 lb pre-cooked
   couscous semolina
1 small dried hot red pepper
1 tbsp caraway seeds
Ground coriander
1 tsp paprika
Parsley
Olive oil

Servings: 4	
Preparation time: 15'	
Cooking time: 30'	
Difficulty: ●	
Flavor: ● ● ●	
Kcal (per serving): 302	
Protein (per serving): 6	
Fat (per serving): 16	
Nutritional value: ● ●	

1 Bring the tomato purée and 4–5 tablespoons oil slowly to a boil in a saucepan.

2 In a food mixer, process the hot pepper, the peeled garlic, the caraway seeds, and a pinch of salt. Add to the tomato purée.

3 Add 1 tablespoon ground coriander and the paprika. Simmer the sauce for 15 minutes.

4 Add ¹/2 liter (4 cups) water. When the liquid returns to the boil, pour in the couscous semolina, while stirring, and cook for 5 minutes longer. Dust with ground coriander and minced parsley; serve immediately.

BALIK ÇORBASI

Turkish Fish Soup

200 g/¹/₄ lb grouper
200 g/¹/₄ lb sapphirine gurnard
200 g/¹/₄ lb scorpion fish
1 onion
2 tomatoes
1 green pepper
1 egg, beaten
1 hot red pepper
Olive oil

Servings: 4	
Preparation time: 35′	
Cooking time: 25′	
Difficulty: ●●	
Flavor: ●●	
Kcal (per serving): 284	
Protein (per serving): 31	
Fat (per serving): 14	
Nutritional value: ●●	

1 Clean the fish, scale, rinse, and cut into chunks. Boil for about 15 minutes in slightly salted boiling water. Strain the broth and reserve.

2 Sauté the minced onion with 2 tablespoons oil until transparent. Remove the stems, seeds, and white fibrous membranes from the green pepper; mince. Add, with the diced tomatoes, to the onions.

3 Simmer for 7–8 minutes. Adjust the salt and add the crushed red pepper. Add the fish and the strained broth and cook for 5 minutes longer, stirring frequently.

4 Remove the pan from the heat and add the beaten egg slowly, while stirring.
Serve the soup hot, with or without bread.

Antalya, an important tourist center on the Mediterranean coast of Turkey.

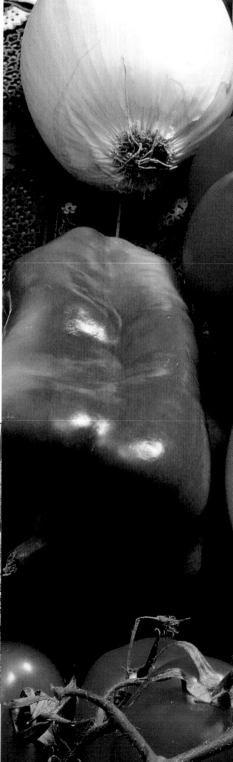

ZUPPA DI SAN GIUSEPPE

Legume Soup

200 g/²/₃ cup dried fava beans
100 g/¹/₂ cup dried peas
100 g/²/₃ cup dried chickpeas
100 g/¹/₂ cup dried white beans
100 g/¹/₂ cup lentils
1 onion
2 dried tomatoes
2 bunches young borage
Fennel seeds
Wild fennel tips
Sliced day-old bakery bread
Olive oil

Servings: 6	
Preparation time: 10'+ 5-6h	
Cooking time: 2h	
Difficulty: ●	
Flavor: ● ●	
Kcal (per serving): 433	
Protein (per serving): 9	
Fat (per serving): 16	
Nutritional value: ● ●	

Soak all the dry legumes (except the lentils) for 5–6 hours. Drain and place, together with the lentils, in a long pot. Cover with cold salted water and simmer for about 2 hours. After 1 hour, add the onion, sliced thinly lengthwise, the borage leaves, a pinch of fennel seeds, the wild fennel, and the tomatoes broken into pieces. When the legumes are cooked, adjust salt and pepper if necessary. Drizzle with olive oil and serve with bread croutons browned in olive oil.

MEATS

3

ARNAKI ME AGHINARES

Lamb and Artichokes

Trim the artichokes, eliminating the outer leaves and cutting off the toughest part of the tops. Leave just a small piece of stem. Cut in half lengthwise, remove the choke, and place in cold water acidulated with the juice of 1 lemon.

1 Melt the butter in a deep pan and sauté the dried lamb pieces until golden. Add the minced onion and cook over moderate heat for a few minutes. Sprinkle with flour, stir, and add water to cover. Bring to a gentle boil. Add 1 tablespoon each minced parsley and dill, two tablespoons lemon juice, and salt and pepper to taste.

2 Drain and dry the artichokes and lay them over the lamb in the pan. Cover and simmer for about 1 hour, adding water as needed. Allow to cool for a few minutes while you beat the egg with the remaining lemon juice. Mix in a few spoonfuls of the warm meat liquor, then pour the egg mixture into the pan. Stir well and reheat: do not allow to boil. Serve hot dusted with minced parsley and dill.

800 g/1 ¾ lbs leg of lamb,
   boned and diced
8 small artichokes
1 onion
2 eggs
Juice of 2 lemons
40 g/3 tbsp butter

Flour
Parsley
Dill

Servings: 4
Preparation time: 20'
Cooking time: 1h 15'
Difficulty: ● ●
Flavor: ● ●
Kcal (per serving): 434
Protein (per serving): 10
Fat (per serving): 55
Nutritional value: ● ●

AGNELLO IN CASSERUOLA

Casseroled Lamb

1 kg/1 ¼ lbs lamb shoulder,
    boned and cut into chunks
600 g/1 ½ lbs new potatoes
1 onion
2-3 cloves garlic
Parsley
Hard pecorino cheese, grated
60 g/2 oz fresh pecorino cheese
Chicken broth
Lard
Olive oil

Servings: 4	
Preparation time: 30'	
Cooking time: 1h 20'	
Difficulty: ● ●	
Flavor: ● ● ●	
Kcal (per serving): 675	
Protein (per serving): 50	
Fat (per serving): 39	
Nutritional value: ● ●	

1 In a casserole, gently sauté the onion, sliced lengthwise, in 4–5 tablespoons olive oil. As soon as it begins to color, add 1 tablespoon lard, the garlic, 1 tablespoon minced parsley, and the lamb.

2 Sauté until the meat is lightly and uniformly colored. Add salt and pepper to taste, and about 1 cup broth.

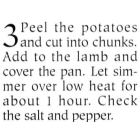

3 Peel the potatoes and cut into chunks. Add to the lamb and cover the pan. Let simmer over low heat for about 1 hour. Check the salt and pepper.

4 Five minutes before serving, add the flaked fresh pecorino cheese and up to $1/2$ cup grated cheese. Stir to blend in the cheese, remove from the heat, and serve immediately.

To prepare beef or chicken broth, you will need about 500 g/1 pound of meat, one carrot, one onion, and one stalk of celery. Place the meat in a pot with about 2 liters/2 quarts cold water; add the vegetables cut into chunks and a pinch of salt. Cover and boil gently for about 2 1/2 hours. Strain before using.

Agneau à l'Étouffée

Stewed Lamb with Beans

1 Soak the beans for 5–6 hours before beginning. Flatten the lamb chops slightly and rub with garlic on both sides. Place in a bowl with a pinch of salt, pepper, and a few tablespoons olive oil. Allow to stand for the time required for soaking the beans.

2 Drain the beans and cook covered in slightly salted water over very low heat for about 1/2 hour. Clean the artichokes, removing the stems and the tougher leaves and tips, and cut crosswise into rounds. Blanch for 5–6 minutes in slightly salted water acidulated with lemon juice.

3 Cut the bacon into strips and fry with 4–5 tablespoons olive oil. Add the lamb chops, a bay leaf, a pinch of nutmeg, the minced carrot and celery, the green onions cut into rounds, and about 1/2 cup tomato purée. Adjust the salt and pepper.

4 Pour over two cups of wine, cover, and simmer for about 2 hours. Add the beans, the artichokes, and about 1/2 cup vegetable broth. Check the salt and pepper and cook for 30 minutes longer.

1 kg/2 1/2 lbs lamb chops
120 g/1/4 lb fatty bacon or lard
200 g/1/2 lb dry white beans
4 violetto artichokes
1 carrot
1 stalk celery
3 green onions
2 cloves garlic

Bay leaf, nutmeg
Tomato purée
1/2 lemon
Dry white wine
Olive oil
Vegetable broth (see p. 44)

Servings: 6

Preparation time: 25' + 5-6h

Cooking time: 2h 45'

Difficulty: ● ●

Flavor: ● ●

Kcal (per serving): 731

Protein (per serving): 45

Fat (per serving): 34

Nutritional value: ● ●

CONIGLIO ALLA CACCIATORA

Rabbit Hunter Style

1 rabbit, 1.2 kg ca/ca. 2 1/2 lbs	
1 onion	
1 stalk celery	
1 clove garlic	
Capers packed in salt	
Green olives in brine	
Parsley	
Tomato paste	
Flour	
Dry Marsala wine	
Olive oil	

Servings: 4	
Preparation time: 25' + 2 h	
Cooking time: 1h	
Difficulty: ● ●	
Flavor: ● ● ●	
Kcal (per serving): 527	
Protein (per serving): 42	
Fat (per serving): 23	
Nutritional value: ● ●	

Rinse and dry the rabbit; cut into pieces. Marinate for about 2 hours in 2 cups Marsala wine.

1 In a deep pan, sauté the onion, sliced lengthwise, in 4–5 tablespoons olive oil with the garlic minced with a few tablespoons parsley. Dredge the rabbit pieces in seasoned flour and brown in the same pan.

2 Add about 2 teaspoons tomato paste diluted in 1 cup hot water; simmer for about 1/2 hour.

3 Add 1 tablespoon capers (rinsed to remove all the salt), the chopped celery, 1/4 cup or more olives, and 1/2 cup of the marinade. Allow to simmer for another 1/2 hour, adding marinade as necessary.

2

1

3

LAPIN À LA PROVENÇALE

Rabbit Provençal

Wash and dry the rabbit; cut into 10–12 pieces. Heat 4 tablespoons olive oil and sauté the rabbit pieces until golden brown; remove and salt lightly. Drain the oil from the pan and pour in 1 cup broth. Warm over moderate heat. Dust the rabbit pieces with flour and add to the broth; after a few minutes, add 1 cup wine, salt and pepper.

Add the seeded, diced tomatoes, the garlic, a few peppercorns, and $\frac{1}{2}$ teaspoon mustard. Cook the rabbit over very low heat, adding more broth if necessary, until tender (about 50 minutes cooking time in all). Strain the sauce and pour it over the rabbit pieces arranged on a serving platter. Serve with green beans and salad.

1 rabbit, 1.3 kg/2 $\frac{1}{2}$ – 3 lbs
3 ripe tomatoes
2 cloves garlic
Prepared mustard
Flour
Dry white wine
Olive oil
Vegetable broth (see p. 44)
Black peppercorns

Servings:	4
Preparation time:	25′ + 2h
Cooking time:	50′
Difficulty:	● ●
Flavor:	● ●
Kcal (per serving):	468
Protein (per serving):	46
Fat (per serving):	18
Nutritional value:	● ●

MAIALE IN CROSTA

Pork en Croûte

350 g/3 cups flour
15 g/¹/₂ oz compressed yeast
700 g/1 ¹/₂ lbs ground pork
Grated pecorino cheese
Parsley
Juice of 1 lemon
Lard, olive oil

Servings: 4	
Preparation time: 25' + 1h	
Cooking time: 30'	
Difficulty: ● ●	
Flavor: ● ●	
Kcal (per serving): 816	
Protein (per serving): 47	
Fat (per serving): 37	
Nutritional value: ● ● ●	

1 Dissolve the yeast in few tablespoons warm water; mix the dissolved yeast into the flour with a drop of olive oil and a pinch of salt. Form into a ball and allow to rest for about 1 hour. In a bowl, mix the ground pork with 1 tablespoon minced parsley, salt, pepper, the lemon juice, and about ¹/₂ cup grated pecorino cheese.

2 Roll out the dough to form a disk about ¹/₂ cm (¹/₄ inch) thick; grease the top side of the disk with lard and place the filling on one half. Fold over the other side of the disk (like a calzone) and seal the edges. Grease the top of the crust lightly with lard and bake in a 200°C/375–400°F oven for about 30 minutes.

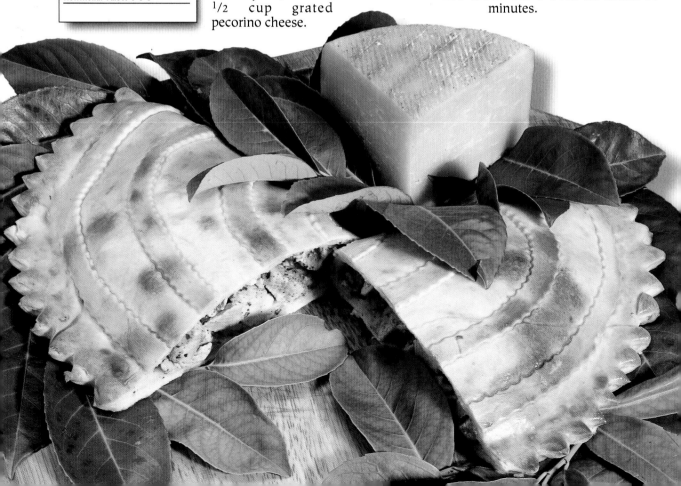

Scaloppine al Finocchio

Veal Cutlets with Fennel

600–700 g/1 $\frac{1}{2}$ lbs veal cutlets (loin or rump)
Wild fennel seeds
Flour
Vegetable broth (see p. 44)
Dry white wine
30 g/2 tbsp butter
Olive oil

Servings: 4	
Preparation time: 10'	
Cooking time: 20'	
Difficulty: ●	
Flavor: ●	
Kcal (per serving): 400	
Protein (per serving): 23	
Fat (per serving): 28	
Nutritional value: ● ●	

Vegetable broth (see p. 44)

Positano, one of the pearls of Italy's Amalfi coast.

Season the veal cutlets with salt and pepper and dust with flour. Cook over medium heat for about 15 minutes in 3 tablespoons olive oil and 1 tablespoon butter.

Arrange the meat on a heated serving platter and keep warm while you prepare the sauce. Remove some of the excess fat from the pan. While stirring over low heat, add 1 tablespoon butter and about 1 teaspoon fennel seeds. Add $\frac{1}{2}$ cup wine and evaporate over high heat; add $\frac{1}{2}$ cup broth and simmer over low heat for a few minutes. Pour the sauce over the cutlets and serve.

Wild fennel (or finocchietto, as it is called in some regions of Italy) is the progenitor of cultivated fennel. It is one of the most common aromatic herbs in the Mediterranean region, where it grows wild almost everywhere.
The sun-dried seeds and fruits are widely used in both cooking and in preserving and flavoring meats.

DOLMADAKIA

Stuffed Grape Leaves

20 grape leaves
300 g/^{3}/$_4$ lb ground beef
^{1}/$_2$ cup rice
1 small onion
Juice of 1 lemon
2 tbsp minced parsley
2 tbsp butter
1 egg

Servings: 4	
Preparation time: 20'	
Cooking time: 1h 10'	
Difficulty: ● ●	
Flavor: ● ●	
Kcal (per serving): 336	
Protein (per serving): 32	
Fat (per serving): 19	
Nutritional value: ●	

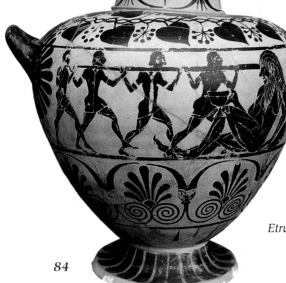

Blanch the grape leaves for 5 minutes; lay out on a cloth to cool. Cook the rice in boiling salted water; drain. In a bowl, mix the ground meat, the rice, the finely diced onion, and the parsley. Salt and pepper to taste. Place a heaping tablespoon of filling at one end of each grape leaf; roll up and seal the ends. Place the filled leaves in a deep pan (overlapping if necessary). Add the butter and 2 cups water. Place a weighted plate over the top to prevent the leaves from unrolling during cooking. Simmer over low to medium heat for about 50 minutes.

Beat the egg with the lemon juice and a few tablespoons of the cooking liquor. Pour back into the pan over the grape leaf rolls. As soon as the liquid begins to bubble again, remove from the heat and serve.

Etruscan vase illustrating the blinding of Polyphemus, from the Odyssey.

BŒUF EN DAUBE

Casseroled Beef

1 Peel the onions. Stud one with the cloves; cut both into wedges. Peel the carrot and cut into chunks. Prepare the bouquet garni with the rinsed and trimmed herbs.

2 Cut the bacon into strips and cook in a deep frying pan in 4 tablespoons olive oil with the onions, the carrot, the tomato purée, the garlic, the bouquet garni, the orange peel, a pinch of salt, and a few peppercorns. After 5–6 minutes, add the beef, cut into chunks, and enough red wine to cover. Cover the pan and bring to a boil over high heat; lower the heat and simmer very slowly, covered, for at least 2-1/2 hours. Add wine as necessary; adjust salt and pepper.

800 g/1 ³/4 lbs stew beef
80 g/3 oz fatty bacon or lard
200 g/1 cup tomato purée
2 onions
1 carrot
4 cloves garlic
1 bouquet garni (thyme, sage,
   bay leaf, rosemary, parsley)
¹/2 tsp grated orange peel
3-4 cloves
Black peppercorns
Red wine
Olive oil

Servings: 4	
Preparation time: 15′	
Cooking time: 2h 40′	
Difficulty: ● ●	
Flavor: ● ●	
Kcal (per serving): 491	
Protein (per serving): 43	
Fat (per serving): 25	
Nutritional value: ● ●	

MALFUF MAHSHI

Cabbage Rolls

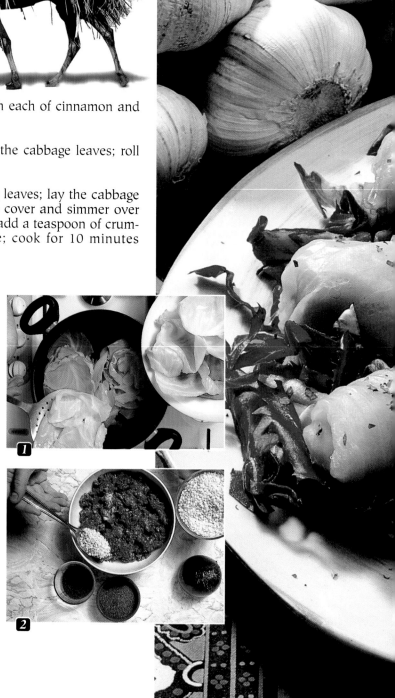

1 Separate the cabbage leaves and wash; blanch for 4 minutes in slightly salted water. Drain and remove the tough rib.

2 In a bowl, mix the meat, the rinsed rice, the minced onion, a pinch of salt and pepper, and a pinch each of cinnamon and paprika.

3 Place the filling by tablespoons on the cabbage leaves; roll and seal.

4 Line a deep pan with the remaining leaves; lay the cabbage rolls on the leaf base. Add water to cover and simmer over medium heat. After about 35 minutes, add a teaspoon of crumbled dried mint and the lemon juice; cook for 10 minutes longer. Serve immediately.

---

1 white cabbage
500 g/1 lb ground beef or lamb
100 g/²/₃ cup rice
1 onion
Juice of 2 lemons
Dried mint
Ground cinnamon
Paprika

Servings: 4	
Preparation time: 35′	
Cooking time: 50′	
Difficulty: ● ●	
Flavor: ● ●	
Kcal (per serving): 284	
Protein (per serving): 37	
Fat (per serving): 2	
Nutritional value: ●	

SCALOPPE ALLA CAPRESE

Veal Cutlets Capri Style

550 g/1–1 1/4 lbs sliced veal rump
Capers in vinegar
2 cloves garlic
Dry white wine
Parsley
30 g/2 tbsp butter
Olive oil

Servings: 4

Preparation time: 10'

Cooking time: 20'

Difficulty: ● ●

Flavor: ● ●

Kcal (per serving): 282

Protein (per serving): 28

Fat (per serving): 18

Nutritional value: ●

This is a quick, tasty main course. What to serve as a vegetable?
Boil 600 g/1 1/2 pounds trimmed green beans in slightly salted water for 15 minutes. Mince 2 cloves garlic and a good-sized bunch of parsley. Add to the drained beans with 1 tablespoon drained capers, olive oil, salt, and pepper. Toss and serve. A perfect side dish.

Separate the parsley leaves from the stalks; wash, dry, and mince the leaves. Melt the butter in a frying pan with 3–4 tablespoons olive oil. Lightly brown the cutlets on both sides; add salt and pepper to taste. Drain and keep warm. In another pan, sauté the garlic lightly in 3–4 tablespoons olive oil.

Remove as soon as it begins to color; add 3 tablespoons drained capers to the oil. Pour over 1 cup wine and evaporate over low heat. Add the meat and simmer for 5 minutes; remove from the heat. Place the cutlets on a serving platter; pour over the caper sauce and sprinkle with minced parsley.

550 g/1–1 1/4 lbs veal rump cutlets
3 ripe tomatoes
1 shallot
1 stalk celery
2 cloves garlic
Black olives preserved with garlic
Parsley
Hot red pepper
Dry white wine
30 g/2 tbsp butter
Olive oil

Servings:	4
Preparation time:	15'
Cooking time:	35'
Difficulty:	● ●
Flavor:	● ● ●
Kcal (per serving):	345
Protein (per serving):	29
Fat (per serving):	23
Nutritional value:	●

SCALOPPE ALLA SICILIANA

Veal Cutlets Sicilian Style

Wash and dry the tomatoes; cut in half lengthwise. Remove the seeds and cut into chunks. Cut the olives in half and remove the pits, leaving a few whole for garnish.

Melt the butter in a frying pan with 3–4 tablespoons olive oil. Lightly brown the cutlets on both sides; salt and pepper to taste. Drain and keep warm.

Trim and chop the celery with the peeled garlic and shallot; sauté until just transparent in 4 tablespoons olive oil with two crushed hot pepper cases (remove the seeds) and a pinch of salt. Pour over 1/2 cup wine and cook until evaporated.

Add the tomatoes and the pitted olives and simmer over medium heat for about 10 minutes, adding a tablespoon or two of water should the sauce thicken too much. Add the meat and simmer for 4–5 minutes. Serve the meat smothered in the tasty sauce. Garnish the serving platter with whole black olives and sprigs of parsley.

A picturesque, brightly-painted Sicilian cart.

89

VITELLO IN FALSOMAGRO

Stuffed Rolled Roast

500 g/1 lb beef or veal rump
  (1 wide slice)
Tomato sauce (see p. 31)
Red wine
Lard (optional)
Olive oil

For the stuffing
1 sausage
140 g/5–6 oz sliced prosciutto
  ham
60 g/2-3 oz ground beef
70 g/3 oz bacon
1 egg plus 2 hard-boiled eggs
1 green onion
1 clove garlic
80 g/3 oz (ca. $1/3$ cup) shelled
  peas
80 g/3 oz sharp *caciocavallo* or
  provolone cheese
Pecorino cheese with
  peppercorns, grated
Parsley

Servings: 4	
Preparation time: 40'	
Cooking time: 1h 15'	
Difficulty: ●●●	
Flavor: ●●●	
Kcal (per serving): 1069	
Protein (per serving): 64	
Fat (per serving): 77	
Nutritional value: ●●●	

1 Flatten the meat into the closest possible approximation of a uniform rectangle. Cover with slices of prosciutto and boiled egg slices.

2 Arrange strips of bacon and *cacio-cavallo* (or provolone) cheese lengthwise on the meat; sprinkle with minced garlic, parsley leaves, and the sliced green onion.

3 In a bowl, blend the ground beef, the beaten egg, 1/4–1/2 cup grated pecorino cheese, the peas, the crumbled sausage, and salt and pepper to taste. Spread the mixture evenly over the meat.

4 Roll the roast and tie tightly with kitchen twine. Sauté in 3–4 tablespoons olive oil and 1 tablespoon lard (optional), turning frequently until uniformly browned. Pour in 1 cup wine and evaporate over high heat; reduce the heat and add about 1 cup tomato sauce diluted with a little water. Cover and simmer for about 1 hour, adding liquid if necessary.

Before serving, untie the roast and slice. Serve with the sauce on the side.

91

POLLO AL CHILINDRÓN

Chicken in Chilindròn Sauce

1 Clean and dress the chicken; cut into a dozen or so small pieces, and brown over high heat for 5–6 minutes in 2–3 tablespoons olive oil. Trim and if desired seed the tomatoes; remove the stems, seeds, and white fibrous membranes from the peppers; cut both ingredients into pieces.

2 Sauté the minced onion and garlic in 3–4 tablespoons olive oil in a deep frying pan. Add the tomatoes and sweet peppers. Cook over medium heat for about 10 minutes.

3 Add the browned chicken pieces and simmer for about 10 minutes.

4 Add the prosciutto cut into strips. Pour over 1 cup wine and simmer for 5 minutes. Raise the heat and boil until the wine evaporates. Serve the chicken in the sauce.
A warm-weather suggestion: use only one-half chicken and double the quantity of tomatoes and peppers. Serve warm or cold with white rice.

1 chicken, 1 kg/2–2 1/2 lbs
120 g/1/4 lb prosciutto ham
4–5 ripe tomatoes
2 sweet peppers
1 onion
1 clove garlic
Hot red pepper
Red wine
Olive oil

Servings:	4
Preparation time:	20'
Cooking time:	30'
Difficulty:	●●
Flavor:	●●●
Kcal (per serving):	522
Protein (per serving):	36
Fat (per serving):	39
Nutritional value:	●●

POLLO AL SALE

Chicken in Salt Crust

1 chicken, 1.2 kg/ca. 2 1/2 lbs	
Coarse salt, 3 kg/ca. 6 lbs	
Servings: 4	
Preparation time: 15'	
Cooking time: 1h 15'	
Difficulty: ●	
Flavor: ● ●	
Kcal (per serving): 310	
Protein (per serving): 22	
Fat (per serving): 22	
Nutritional value: ●	

Clean and dress the chicken. Cover the bottom of an oven-proof dish or baking pan with about 1 kg (2 lbs) of the salt. Place the chicken in the dish and cover with the rest of the salt. Cover the dish tightly and tie or weight the cover. Bake in a 180–200°C/350–375°F oven for about 1 1/4 hours.

Break the crust and extract the chicken. Remove every trace of salt. We suggest carving this tender, delicious bird at the table.

POULET À L'AIL

Garlic Chicken

Preheat the oven to 180°C/350°F. Clean and dry the chicken; salt and pepper the cavity and fill with exactly half of the minced herbs (sage, thyme, rosemary). Tie tightly and place in a baking pan. Pour over 2 tablespoons olive oil and sprinkle with the other half of the herbs.

Separate the cloves of garlic, but do not peel. Place all around the chicken, together with the sliced celery. Drizzle with 2 tablespoons olive oil. Bake for 15 minutes, then add 1/2 cup hot broth and continue baking for another hour, basting occasionally.

Serve the chicken with toasted whole wheat bread, on which you may spread the garlic cooked in its "shirt."

1 chicken, 1.8 kg/ca. 2 lbs
4 heads garlic
2 stalks celery
1 sprig fresh sage
4 sprigs thyme
2 sprigs rosemary
Chicken broth
Toasted whole wheat bread
Olive oil

Servings: 6	
Preparation time: 15'	
Cooking time: 1h 15'	
Difficulty: ●	
Flavor: ● ●	
Kcal (per serving): 653	
Protein (per serving): 42	
Fat (per serving): 50	
Nutritional value: ● ●	

PIRINCLI PILIC

Chicken and Rice Turkish Style

1 chicken, 1.2 kg ca/ca. 2 1/2 lbs
250 g/1 1/3 cups rice
60 g/4 tbsp butter
1 onion
1/4 cup raisins
1/4 cup pine nuts
Chicken broth

Servings: 4	
Preparation time: 45′	
Cooking time: 50′	
Difficulty: ● ●	
Flavor: ● ●	
Kcal (per serving): 613	
Protein (per serving): 31	
Fat (per serving): 35	
Nutritional value: ● ●	

Clean and dress the chicken; cut into pieces. Reserve the liver and dice.

1 Cover the rice with warm water and let stand for 1/2 hour; drain. Soak the raisins for 1/2 hour; drain and squeeze dry. If necessary, remove the dark skin from the pine nuts.

2 Melt half of the butter in a deep frying pan and brown the chicken with the coarsely-sliced onion and the liver.

3 Add the raisins, and salt to taste. Pour in 2 cups broth and cook over medium heat for 1/2 hour.

4 When the chicken has cooked for 1/2 hour, melt the rest of the butter in another pan and toast the rice with the pine nuts. Add 2 cups hot broth, cover, and simmer over low heat for 20 minutes (adding broth if necessary) while the chicken continues to cook.
Make a bed of the rice on a serving platter and top with the chicken pieces and their sauce.

POLLO IN SALSA

Chicken in Mint and Parsley Sauce

1 chicken, 1.2 kg/ca. 2 $^1/_2$ lbs
Flour (optional)
Olive oil

For the sauce
Fresh mint, parsley, garlic
Vinegar
Olive oil

Servings: 4	
Preparation time: 30' + 30'	
Cooking time: 45'	
Difficulty: ●	
Flavor: ● ●	
Kcal (per serving): 684	
Protein (per serving): 35	
Fat (per serving): 54	
Nutritional value: ● ●	

Prepare the mint and parsley sauce. In a food blender, chop the leaves of a large bunch of fresh mint, a handful of parsley, and one clove garlic. Process at low speed until reduced to a pulp. Add 6 tablespoons olive oil and the same amount of vinegar. Mix well; adjust salt and pepper. Allow to stand for at least 30 minutes before using.

Clean and dress the chicken; cut into pieces. Season with salt and pepper and a little olive oil; grill the pieces over charcoal or in the oven broiler. Or you may lightly flour the pieces and fry in 4–5 tablespoons oil. Serve the chicken hot with the mint and parsley herb sauce on the side.

1 lobster, 1.2 kg/ca. 1 1/2 lbs
3 sweet peppers (red, green, yellow)
1 bouquet garni (tarragon, parsley, thyme)
1 tbsp each: pickled baby gherkins, baby onions, and capers
2 anchovies
Parsley
Olive oil

Servings: 4
Preparation time: 30′
Cooking time: 30′
Difficulty: ● ●
Flavor: ● ● ●
Kcal (per serving): 342
Protein (per serving): 34
Fat (per serving): 19
Nutritional value: ●

BRANZINO AL SALE

Sea Bass in Salt Crust

1 sea bass, 1 kg/ca. 2 1/4 lbs
Coarse salt

Servings:	4
Preparation time:	15'
Cooking time:	2h 30'
Difficulty:	●
Flavor:	● ●
Kcal (per serving):	155
Protein (per serving):	31
Fat (per serving):	3
Nutritional value:	●

Clean the fish and remove the entrails, but do not scale. Rinse and dry thoroughly.

Cover the bottom of a suitably-sized deep baking pan with about 1.5 cm (1/2 inch) of salt. Lay the fish on the salt. Do not add any seasoning.

Cover the fish with more salt, taking care that it is covered by at least 1.5 cm (1/2 inch). Bake in a preheated slow to moderate (160°C/300–350°F) for at least 2 1/2 hours.

At the end of cooking time the salt should have formed a solid block with a brown crust.

Break the crust with an ice-pick or the point of a large knife. Extract the fish and remove all residual salt.

This ancient, time-proven method of cookery guarantees flavorful, tender, and fragrant meats.

LSTERIA (VLACHOS) ME SALZA TOMATA

Grouper with Tomatoes

Lay the fish steaks (1.5 cm/^{1}/$_2$ inch thickness) in the bottom of an oiled baking pan. Cover with the sliced onions. Sprinkle with salt and pepper and 1 cup wine.

In a bowl, mix the tomato purée with ^{1}/$_2$ cup olive oil; add salt and pepper to taste. Pour half the mixture over the fish.

Mince the garlic with the parsley leaves (^{1}/$_4$ cup or more) and mix in 6 tablespoons breadcrumbs. Sprinkle half this mixture over the fish. Cover the entire surface with the sliced tomatoes, the remaining purée mixture, and the remaining breadcrumb mixture, in that order. Bake at 200°C/375°F for 40 minutes.

1.5 kg/3 lbs grouper steaks
500 g/1 lb white onions
1 cup tomato purée
White wine
Fine dry breadcrumbs
500 g/1 lb fresh tomatoes
3 cloves garlic
1 bunch parsley
Olive oil

Servings: 6	
Preparation time: 15′	
Cooking time: 40′	
Difficulty: ●	
Flavor: ● ●	
Kcal (per serving): 356	
Protein (per serving): 35	
Fat (per serving): 16	
Nutritional value: ●	

CALAMARI RIPIENI

Stuffed Calamari Squid

6 medium calamari squid
(7–800 g/1 1/2 – 1 3/4 lbs
total weight)
Fine dry breadcrumbs
1 clove garlic
Parsley
100 g/1/4 lb Sicilian *toma* (or
other low-fat cow's milk
cheese)
Oregano
Olive oil

Servings: 4

Preparation time: 25'

Cooking time: 45'

Difficulty: ● ●

Flavor: ● ●

Kcal (per serving): 382

Protein (per serving): 33

Fat (per serving): 21

Nutritional value: ●

1 Clean the squid, removing the eyes and the beak. Mince the heads and tentacles. Toast 1 cup or more breadcrumbs in a little olive oil; add the mince and cook for a few minutes.

2 Remove from heat and mix in the garlic, minced with about 1/4 cup parsley; add salt and pepper to taste. Mix in the diced cheese.

3 Stuff the squid with this mixture. "Pin" the tops closed with tooth-picks. Place in a lightly greased baking pan and bake at 180°C/350°F for about 30 minutes, basting occasionally with a sprig of oregano dipped in olive oil seasoned with salt and pepper.

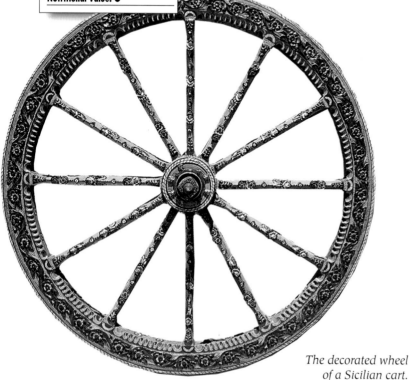

The decorated wheel of a Sicilian cart.

MEJILLONES RELLENOS

Stuffed Mussels

1.5 kg/3 ½ lbs mussels
1 sweet red pepper
1 clove garlic
1 onion
Parsley
Dry white wine
Olive oil

Servings: 4	
Preparation time: 30'	
Cooking time: 15'	
Difficulty: ●	
Flavor: ●●●	
Kcal (per serving): 146	
Protein (per serving): 6	
Fat (per serving): 6	
Nutritional value: ●	

Scrub the mussels repeatedly under running water; remove the beards. Rinse the pepper, remove the stem, seeds, and white fibrous membranes, and dice finely.

Heat 2 tablespoons olive oil over low heat; add the diced pepper, the garlic, and the sliced onion. Cook without browning for 3–4 minutes. Add the mussels, 1 cup wine, and a tablespoon minced parsley. Cover and simmer until the mussels open. Remove from heat. Discard the empty half-shell of each mussel; arrange the mussels on the half-shell on a serving platter. Strain the contents of the pan, reserving the cooking liquid. Top each mussel with a spoonful of the strained mixture. Taste the filtered juice; add salt and freshly-ground pepper to taste. Pour the liquid over the mussels. As a final touch, sprinkle the platter with fresh minced parsley.

DENTICE AL FORNO

Baked Dentex

| 1 dentex or sea bream, 1.3 kg/2 1/2 – 3 lbs |
| 1 onion |
| 4 potatoes |
| Capers packed in salt |
| Green olives |
| Hot red pepper, rosemary, thyme |
| Beef broth |
| Olive oil |

Servings: 4	
Preparation time: 20′	
Cooking time: 45′	
Difficulty: ● ●	
Flavor: ● ●	
Kcal (per serving): 499	
Protein (per serving): 41	
Fat (per serving): 23	
Nutritional value: ●	

Remove the entrails and clean the fish. Mince the onion. Season the inside of the fish with a dash of salt and stuff with a sprig of thyme, rosemary, and half the onion. Sauté the remaining onion until soft in 3–4 tablespoons olive oil with the peeled and diced potatoes, 1/2 crushed hot red pepper, 1/4 cup or more pitted olives, and 2 tablespoons rinsed capers.

Transfer the vegetables to a baking dish. Lay the seasoned fish on top and pour over 1 to 1 1/2 cups broth.

Bake in a preheated 180–190°C/350–375°F oven for about 30 minutes, basting occasionally and adding more broth as needed.

GARIDES STO FOURNO

Shrimp Greek Style

10–12 jumbo shrimp, prawns,
  or langoustines
250 g/1/2 lb hard feta cheese
4 ripe tomatoes
2 medium onions
1 sweet pepper
2 clove garlic
100 g/1/4 lb green olives
Parsley
Ground hot red pepper
Olive oil

Servings: 4	
Preparation time: 30'	
Cooking time: 45'	
Difficulty: ●●	
Flavor: ●●●	
Kcal (per serving): 549	
Protein (per serving): 35	
Fat (per serving): 39	
Nutritional value: ●●	

1

3

2

4

1 Peel the onions and cut into thin slices; remove the stem, seeds, and white fibrous membranes from the pepper and cut lengthwise into thin strips. Sauté both ingredients until soft, in 4–5 tablespoons olive oil, with the garlic.

2 Add the cleaned, seeded, and diced tomatoes and a pinch of salt and pepper. Simmer for 10–12 minutes.

3 Rinse and dry the shrimp. Arrange in a single layer in a baking dish. Cover with the tomato mixture.

4 Sprinkle with crumbled feta cheese, the olives, a dash of hot red pepper, and minced parsley. Bake in a preheated 180°C/350°F oven for about 30 minutes. Serve immediately.

MAZZANCOLLE ALLA ROMANA

Prawns Roman Style

16–20 *mazzancolle* ("Imperial" prawns)
3–4 ripe tomatoes
1 shallot
1 clove garlic
Fine dry breadcrumbs
Parsley
Olive oil

Servings: 4

Preparation time: 30'

Cooking time: 20'

Difficulty: ● ●

Flavor: ● ●

Kcal (per serving): 291

Protein (per serving): 16

Fat (per serving): 16

Nutritional value: ●

Mince the shallot with a sprig of parsley. Peel and seed the tomatoes; dice.

Mince the garlic with 2–3 tablespoons parsley; in a bowl, mix with 10 tablespoons breadcrumbs and 4–5 tablespoons olive oil.

Rinse the prawns, dry well, and shell the tail portion (without detaching the head). Dredge in the breadcrumb mixture until uniformly coated. Sauté in 5–6 tablespoons olive oil until golden, turning frequently. Remove from the pan, drain and keep warm on a heated serving platter.

Add the chopped shallot to the oil remaining in the pan and sauté until soft. Add the tomatoes and salt to taste.

Cook the sauce for a few minutes until slightly thickened.

Pour the sauce over the prawns, sprinkle with minced parsley, and drizzle with olive oil just before serving.

MOSCARDINI ALLA LIGURE

Octopus Ligurian Style

Pit the olives. Clean the *moscardini*. Bring the broth, to which you have added salt and 1/4 cup vinegar, to a boil. Add the *moscardini* and boil for 15 minutes. Drain, dry, and cut into pieces. Mince the onion with the garlic; sauté in about 5 tablespoons olive oil with 1 bay leaf, a sprig of thyme, and the hot peppers until the onion is golden. Add the *moscardini* and cook for a few minutes over low heat. Add the olives, salt and pepper to taste, and stir well. Continue to simmer until the *moscardini* are tender, adding broth if necessary.
Serve warm, with the sauce.

These moscardini *can be preserved for future use. After having added the olives, cook for 5 minutes more, then remove from the heat and allow to cool. Boil 1 quart vinegar with bay leaf and thyme. Pack the* moscardini *into Ball jars and cover with the hot vinegar. Screw the caps on tightly and store in a dark, cool place (or in the refrigerator). Use within 4–5 weeks.*

800 g/1 3/4 lbs *moscardini*
 (small octopodes)
24 green olives
1 clove garlic
1 green onion
2 hot red peppers
Bay leaf and thyme
Vegetable broth (see p. 44)
White wine vinegar
Olive oil

Servings: 4	
Preparation time: 25'	
Cooking time: 35' + 30'	
Difficulty: ● ●	
Flavor: ● ● ●	
Kcal (per serving): 228	
Protein (per serving): 16	
Fat (per serving): 16	
Nutritional value: ●	

LORATA AL FINOCCHIETTO

Gilthead with Fennel

1 gilthead, 1 kg/ca. 2 1/4 lbs
1 fennel with leaves
1 potato
2 cloves garlic
Fennel seeds
4 pickled hot green peppers
Parsley
Dry white wine
Olive oil

Servings: 4	
Preparation time: 20' + 2h	
Cooking time: 40'	
Difficulty: ● ● ●	
Flavor: ● ●	
Kcal (per serving): 367	
Protein (per serving): 32	
Fat (per serving): 17	
Nutritional value: ●	

1 Scale the gilthead and remove the entrails; rinse well and dry. Marinate for about 2 hours in 3–4 cups good-quality white wine to which you have added 1 tablespoon olive oil, the hot peppers, and the peeled and crushed garlic. Drain the fish well before seasoning with salt and pepper.

2 Wash the fennel; remove the tougher outer layers and the tops of the larger stems. Reserve the green leaves as garnish. Cut into small pieces and boil in lightly salted water for 5–6 minutes. Remove from the water with a slotted spoon, drain, and chop.

3 Cover the bottom of a well-oiled baking pan with the chopped fennel. Peel and slice the potato; arrange the slices over the fennel, without overlapping.

4 Lay the fish on the bed of potato slices. Sprinkle with the peppers from the marinade, chopped, and drizzle with olive oil. Bake in a preheated 180°C/350°F oven for about 1/2 hour, basting occasionally with a few tablespoons of the marinade.
Serve the fish sprinkled with fennel seeds and surrounded by the vegetables. Garnish the platter with the fennel tops and sprigs of parsley.

Bathing establishments at Sorrento, one of Italy's most elegant and most famous vacation spots.

PAGELLO MARINATO

Marinated Sargo

1 sargo or red bream,
  1 kg ca/ca. 2 1/4 lbs
100 g/1/4 lb lard or fatty bacon
  (in a single slice)
100 g/1/4 lb fontina cheese
150 g/5–6 oz black olives
3–4 cloves garlic
Parsley
1 lemon (as garnish)
White vinegar
Dry white wine
Peppercorns
Olive oil

Servings: 4	
Preparation time: 25' + 2h	
Cooking time: 35'	
Difficulty: ●●●	
Flavor: ●●●	
Kcal (per serving): 899	
Protein (per serving): 33	
Fat (per serving): 74	
Nutritional value: ●●●	

1 Scale the fish and remove the entrails; rinse well and dry. Marinate in 1/2 liter wine to which you have added 1/2 cup vinegar, 3–4 tablespoons olive oil, the garlic, parsley, a pinch of salt, and a tablespoon of peppercorns.

2 After about 2 hours, remove the fish from the marinade and drain well but do not dry. Season the inside of the fish with a pinch of salt and stuff with the diced lard and cheese and the pitted black olives.

3 Sew the opening closed with a strong needle and heavy thread. This operation is rather difficult, but it is essential for good presentation of the dish.

4 Lay the fish on a rectangle of aluminum foil with the herbs from the marinade and a few tablespoons of the liquid. Drizzle with olive oil. Seal the foil around the fish. Place in a baking pan and bake at 200°C/375–400°F for 30 minutes or more. To serve, open the foil packet and garnish the fish with lemon slices and sprigs of parsley.

PESCE SPADA ALL'ACETO

Vinegar Swordfish

4 swordfish steaks
(1 kg/ca. 2 1/4 lbs total weight)
2 ripe tomatoes
1 onion
1 stalk celery
Capers packed in salt
Pitted green olives in brine
Flour
Vinegar
Olive oil

Servings: 4

Preparation time: 15'

Cooking time: 30'

Difficulty: ● ●

Flavor: ● ●

Kcal (per serving): 440

Protein (per serving): 48

Fat (per serving): 22

Nutritional value: ●

Dredge the fish steaks in flour and sauté in 3–4 tablespoons olive oil until golden on both sides. Drain and keep warm.

In another pan, sauté the sliced onion and the finely-chopped celery in 4–5 tablespoons olive oil; add 1 tablespoon rinsed capers, a generous handful of olives (1/2 cup or more), the diced tomatoes, and salt and pepper to taste.

Pour in about 1/3 cup hot water and cook over high heat until the sauce thickens.

Add the fish and 1/2 cup vinegar. Cover and simmer until the vinegar has evaporated. Serve immediately.

PESCE SPADA ALLA GRIGLIA

Grilled Swordfish

Oil and lightly salt the fish; grill for 3–4 minutes per side over hot coals (or under the oven broiler).
Serve immediately with warm oregano sauce, prepared according to the recipe on page 32.

4 swordfish steaks (1 kg ca/ca. 2 $^1/_4$ lbs total weight)

For the oregano sauce
2 lemons
Garlic, oregano, parsley
Olive oil

Servings:	4
Preparation time:	15'
Cooking time:	40'
Difficulty:	● ●
Flavor:	● ●
Kcal (per serving):	435
Protein (per serving):	46
Fat (per serving):	26
Nutritional value:	●

Pesce Spada alla Messinese

Swordfish Messina Style

4 swordfish steaks
  (1 kg/ca. 2 ¼ lbs total weight)
1 onion
4–5 ripe tomatoes
3 potatoes
Capers packed in salt
Green olives in brine
Parsley
Olive oil

Servings: 4	
Preparation time: 20′	
Cooking time: 40′	
Difficulty:	● ●
Flavor:	● ●
Kcal (per serving): 528	
Protein (per serving): 20	
Fat (per serving): 22	
Nutritional value:	●

In a pan large enough to accommodate the swordfish steaks, sauté the sliced onion until soft in 4–5 tablespoons olive oil. Add about a dozen pitted olives, the diced tomatoes, 1 tablespoon rinsed capers, and a dash of salt and pepper. Cover and simmer for about 15 minutes.

Boil the potatoes, skin, and slice or dice.

Lay the swordfish steaks on top of the sauce and the potatoes on the fish; sprinkle with minced parsley. Simmer for 10–15 minutes; adjust the salt and pepper. Serve immediately.

POLPO "MURATO"

Octopus in Terracotta

1 octopus, 1 kg/ca. 2 $^1/_4$ lbs
4–5 ripe tomatoes
$^1/_2$ onion
1 clove garlic
Parsley, hot red pepper
Cuttlefish ink (optional)
Red wine
Olive oil

Servings: 4	
Preparation time: 20'	
Cooking time: 50'	
Difficulty: ● ●	
Flavor: ● ● ●	
Kcal (per serving): 375	
Protein (per serving): 29	
Fat (per serving): 18	
Nutritional value: ●	

Clean the octopus (see page 120). Sauté gently in 3–4 tablespoons olive oil with a mince of parsley, the garlic, and the onion. Add the diced tomatoes, a pinch of salt, 1 hot red pepper, and $^1/_2$ cup red wine. Cover and simmer over very low heat for about 45 minutes, adding a dash of ink near the end of the cooking time, if desired. Allow the octopus to cool somewhat in the sauce before serving, in order to tenderize the meat and bring out the full flavor.

Why the name "murato?" Because tradition calls for cooking the octopus in a hermetically-sealed amphora – "walled in," as it were. But since this sort of recipient is not easy to come by nowadays, we suggest you use a flame-proof terracotta casserole with a tight-fitting cover (and a flame spreader). Tie or weight the cover if necessary. A pressure-cooker also works well – but remember to cut cooking time in half!

POULPE À LA PROVENÇALE

Octopus Provençal

1 octopus, 800g/ca. 1 3/4 lbs
1 clove garlic
1 onion
2 hot red peppers
1 bouquet garni (bay leaf,
  parsley, rosemary, sage)
4–5 ripe tomatoes
New red wine
Olive oil

Servings: 4	
Preparation time: 25' + 20'	
Cooking time: 2h 10'	
Difficulty: ● ●	
Flavor: ● ● ●	
Kcal (per serving): 253	
Protein (per serving): 17	
Fat (per serving): 12	
Nutritional value: ●	

Wash and seed the tomatoes; dice. Place the cleaned octopus in a pot of cold water with a pinch of salt. Heat, covered, over a high flame. When the water boils, reduce the heat and simmer for 1 1/2 hours (30 minutes in a pressure cooker). Allow the octopus to cool in the cooking liquor before draining, drying, and cutting into pieces.

Peel and slice the onion and mince with the peeled garlic. Sauté in 5 tablespoons olive oil until soft. Add the octopus pieces, mix, and add salt to taste. Add 1/2 cup wine and cook over high heat until evaporated; reduce the heat, add the tomatoes and the bouquet garni.

Simmer, covered, for 1/2 hour, adding hot water (or broth) as needed. During the last 5 minutes of cooking time, uncover the pan and allow the sauce to thicken. Remove the bouquet garni before serving the octopus, piping hot. The ideal side dish? Mashed potatoes.

How to clean an octopus
Rinse well. Turn the head inside out and remove all the entrails, including the ink sac. Remove the eyes and the beak (at the center of the tentacles). Rinse thoroughly again to remove all traces of sand.

POULPE À LA TUNISIENNE

Octopus Tunis Style

Wash the tomatoes thoroughly; cut in half, remove the seeds, and dice. Clean the octopus (see p. 120); place in a pot of cold water with a pinch of salt. Heat, covered, over a high flame. When the water boils, reduce the heat and simmer for 1 1/2 hours (30 minutes in a pressure cooker). Allow the octopus to cool in the cooking liquor before draining, drying, and cutting into pieces.

While the octopus is cooking, peel and slice the onion, and mince with the peeled garlic and the washed celery. Sauté until soft in 5 tablespoons olive oil, with the hot peppers broken into pieces.

Add the tomatoes, a pinch of salt, and 1/4 teaspoon powdered saffron.

Mix well and thicken for a few minutes over high heat. Add the octopus and simmer for 10 minutes more. Remove from the heat and add a few leaves each of basil and parsley.

This recipe is of Tunisian origin, and for this reason – in accordance with the Koranic laws – no wine is used. But religious beliefs permitting, let us suggest a tasty "transgression." Add 1/2 cup white wine when you add the octopus to the sauce, and allow it to evaporate: the result is exquisite.

1 octopus, 800 g/ca. 1 3/4 lbs
1 stalk celery
1 onion
1 clove garlic
4–5 ripe tomatoes
2 hot red peppers
Basil and parsley
Saffron
Olive oil

Servings: 4	
Preparation time: 20' + 20'	
Cooking time: 1h 15'	
Difficulty: ● ●	
Flavor: ● ● ●	
Kcal (per serving): 259	
Protein (per serving): 19	
Fat (per serving): 17	
Nutritional value: ●	

SARDE A BECCAFICO

Sardines Sicilian Style

1 Clean the sardines under running water, removing the head, bones, and entrails. Open like a book and drain overlapped on an inclined plate.

2 Toast about 1 cup breadcrumbs in a frying pan with 3–4 tablespoons olive oil. Transfer to a bowl and mix with the rinsed and broken-up anchovies, 4 tablespoons minced parsley, 1/4 cup raisins (previously soaked and squeezed to remove excess liquid), 1/4 cup pine nuts, and salt and pepper.

3 Stuff the sardines with the mixture and close. Arrange in a greased baking dish, separated by fresh bay leaves. Sprinkle with breadcrumbs and drizzle with olive oil and the lemon juice mixed with 1/2 teaspoon sugar. Bake in a preheated 180°C/350°F oven for 30 minutes; serve hot.

Selinunte (Sicily, Italy). The majestic ruins of Temple E, from the 5th century BC. This temple was perhaps dedicated to Hera.

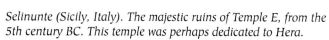

1 kg/2¼ lbs sardines
4 anchovies packed in salt
1 lemon
Fine dry breadcrumbs
Pine nuts
White raisins
Bay leaf

Parsley
Sugar
Olive oil

Servings:	4
Preparation time:	30′
Cooking time:	35′
Difficulty:	● ●
Flavor:	● ● ●
Kcal (per serving):	668
Protein (per serving):	46
Fat (per serving):	34
Nutritional value:	● ●

123

SARDE AL FINOCCHIO

Sardines with Fennel

800 g/1 3/4 lbs sardines
1 onion
350 g/3/4 lb ripe tomatoes
Fennel seeds
Dry white wine
Peppercorns
Olive oil

Servings: 4	
Preparation time: 20'	
Cooking time: 40'	
Difficulty: ● ●	
Flavor: ● ●	
Kcal (per serving): 350	
Protein (per serving): 21	
Fat (per serving): 27	
Nutritional value: ●	

As a vegetable, and as a variation on the theme, we suggest fennel. Cut 2 cultivated fennel bulbs into wedges; boil in slightly salted water until tender. Arrange on the serving platter with the sardines and drizzle with a little extra virgin olive oil and a few drops of vinegar.

Clean the sardines under running water, removing the head, bones, and entrails; fillet. Rinse, seed, and dice the tomatoes. Peel the onion and chop finely.

Sauté the onion over very low heat in 4–5 tablespoons olive oil; when soft, add 1/2 cup wine. Raise the heat until the wine evaporates. Add the tomatoes and a pinch of salt, 2 tablespoons fennel seeds, and a few peppercorns.

Cook the sauce, covered, over low heat for about 20 minutes.

Add the sardines and cook, uncovered, for a scant 10 minutes more over low heat.

Serve the fish smothered with the sauce.

SARDELES MELTEMI

Sardines Meltemi, Greek Style

Rinse a large bunch of parsley and dry it well; mince the leaves finely, together with the garlic. Clean the sardines under running water, removing the head, bones, and entrails; fillet.

Lay the fish in a cooking dish (with a cover) and sprinkle with the minced parsley and garlic, 1/2 cup vinegar, a dash of salt and pepper, and a few tablespoons olive oil. Add the olives.

Cover the dish and place it over another pan of suitable size, filled with water. Bring to a boil and steam for 15 minutes.

Serve the fillets on individual plates, with the olives and other garnishes as desired.

800 g/1 3/4 lbs sardines
Parsley
2 cloves garlic
White wine vinegar
12 black olives
Olive oil

Servings:	4
Preparation time:	20'
Cooking time:	15'
Difficulty:	●
Flavor:	●
Kcal (per serving):	387
Protein (per serving):	21
Fat (per serving):	32
Nutritional value:	●

125

SEPPIE IN INZIMINO

Cuttlefish with Greens

1 kg/2 1/4 lbs medium cuttlefish
2 bunches green chard
   (spinach beet)
2 cloves garlic
300 g/1 1/4 cups tomato purée
Hot red pepper
Dry white wine
Olive oil

Servings: 4	
Preparation time: 15'	
Cooking time: 55'	
Difficulty: ● ●	
Flavor: ● ● ●	
Kcal (per serving): 360	
Protein (per serving): 36	
Fat (per serving): 19	
Nutritional value: ● ●	

1 Clean the cuttlefish following the instructions given below. Cut the body into thickish rings and the tentacles in half.

2 Rinse the greens well, trim and remove the center rib. Blanch in lightly salted water. Drain, squeeze out any excess liquid, and chop coarsely.

3 Sauté the cuttlefish with 3–4 tablespoons olive oil and the garlic; add 1 cup wine and evaporate over high heat; add salt and pepper to taste.

4 Add the greens and simmer for about 10 minutes; add the tomato purée and the hot red pepper and simmer for about 1/2 hour longer.

To clean cuttlefish, separate the body from the tentacles by cutting at the point of attachment; remove the ink sac and the entrails. Cut the inner dorsal side of the body to reveal the bone; widen the opening and pull out the bone. Remove the eyes and the beak (at the center of the ring of tentacles). Rinse the body well both outside and inside, removing all gelatinous portions; rinse the tentacles.

Porto Ercole, on the slopes of the Argentario promontory (Tuscany, Italy).

SGOMBRI AGLI AROMI

Mackerel with Herbs

800 g/1 ¾ lbs mackerel
   (2 fish)
2 cloves garlic
1 lemon
Rosemary
Parsley
Olive oil

Servings: 4	
Preparation time: 20′	
Cooking time: 20′	
Difficulty: ● ●	
Flavor: ● ●	
Kcal (per serving): 373	
Protein (per serving): 22	
Fat (per serving): 30	
Nutritional value: ●	

Mince a large bunch of parsley, rosemary leaves, the garlic, and the rind of ½ lemon.

Wash the mackerel. Eliminate the entrails, skin, and fillet (4 fillets). Lay the fish in an oven-proof dish with 3 tablespoons olive oil. Cover with the minced herbs and sprinkle sparingly with salt and pepper.

Cover the dish with aluminum foil, sealing it around the edges. Bake in a preheated 180°C/350°F oven for about 15 minutes.

Remove the dish from the oven, remove the foil, and drizzle the fillets with extra virgin olive oil before serving with green and red chicory, garnished with lemon slices and sprigs of parsley.

Strictly speaking, "mackerel" refers only to the common mackerel (Scomber scombrus), and not to the other species of this family of fish, more common in the Mediterranean Sea (Scomber colias), known as Spanish or chub mackerel or sgombro lanzardo. Smoked mackerel fillets are the base for an excellent paté to serve as an appetizer on toasted whole wheat bread. In food mixer, process 200 g (½ lb) fillets with 150 g (11 tbsp) butter and the juice and grated rind of 1 lemon, until smooth. This is also an excellent base for caviar canapes.

USKUMRU DOLMASI

Stuffed Mackerel

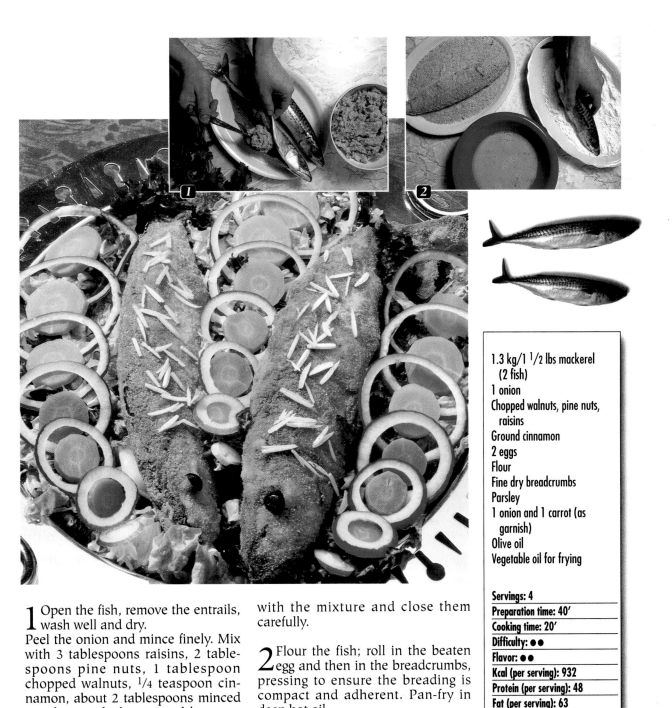

1.3 kg/1 ½ lbs mackerel
   (2 fish)
1 onion
Chopped walnuts, pine nuts,
   raisins
Ground cinnamon
2 eggs
Flour
Fine dry breadcrumbs
Parsley
1 onion and 1 carrot (as
   garnish)
Olive oil
Vegetable oil for frying

Servings:	4
Preparation time:	40'
Cooking time:	20'
Difficulty:	● ●
Flavor:	● ●
Kcal (per serving):	932
Protein (per serving):	48
Fat (per serving):	63
Nutritional value:	● ● ●

1 Open the fish, remove the entrails, wash well and dry.
Peel the onion and mince finely. Mix with 3 tablespoons raisins, 2 tablespoons pine nuts, 1 tablespoon chopped walnuts, ¼ teaspoon cinnamon, about 2 tablespoons minced parsley, and about 1 tablespoon breadcrumbs. Add salt, pepper, and a few teaspoons olive oil. Stuff the fish with the mixture and close them carefully.

2 Flour the fish; roll in the beaten egg and then in the breadcrumbs, pressing to ensure the breading is compact and adherent. Pan-fry in deep hot oil.
Drain and serve cold with onion rings and carrot rounds.

SPIGOLA AL CARTOCCIO

Sea Bass Baked in Foil

1 sea bass, 1.2 kg/ca. 2 1/2 lbs
5–6 ripe tomatoes
Capers packed in salt
Oregano
Olive oil

Servings:	4
Preparation time:	15′
Cooking time:	30′
Difficulty:	● ●
Flavor:	● ●
Kcal (per serving):	378
Protein (per serving):	33
Fat (per serving):	22
Nutritional value:	●

Clean the fish. Lay it on a sheet of oiled aluminum foil with the diced tomatoes, 2 teaspoons oregano, and 1 tablespoon rinsed capers. Sprinkle with salt and pepper.
Seal the foil, place in a baking pan, and bake in a preheated 180°C/350°F oven for about 30 minutes.
Open the foil packet at the table immediately before serving.

TONNO ALLA MARINARA

Tuna Fisherman Style

4 fresh or frozen tuna steaks
   (1 3/4 lbs)
4–5 ripe tomatoes
Fine dry breadcrumbs
Capers packed in salt
Green olives in brine
Fresh mint and parsley
Olive oil

Servings: 4	
Preparation time: 15'	
Cooking time: 30'	
Difficulty: ● ●	
Flavor: ● ● ●	
Kcal (per serving): 448	
Protein (per serving): 45	
Fat (per serving): 21	
Nutritional value: ● ●	

1 Place the tuna steaks in a deep pan with 1 tablespoon rinsed capers, 1/2 cup pitted olives, the diced tomatoes, and salt and pepper to taste. Fill the pan with enough water to almost cover the ingredients.

2 Cook over high heat until the water is almost evaporated. Transfer the fish to a baking dish. Sprinkle with breadcrumbs, minced parsley and mint, and salt and pepper to taste. Drizzle with olive oil. Bake in a 200°C/375–400°F oven for 10 minutes. Serve the fish steaks smothered in the sauce.

THON À LA PROVENÇALE

Tuna Provençal

4 fresh or frozen tuna steaks
   (800 g/1 ³/4 lbs)
4–5 ripe tomatoes
1 onion
2 cloves garlic
1 bouquet garni (bay leaf, wild
   fennel, parsley, thyme)
4 anchovies
Juice of 1 lemon
Dry white wine
Olive oil

Servings: 4	
Preparation time: 20' + 1h	
Cooking time: 1h	
Difficulty: ● ●	
Flavor: ● ● ●	
Kcal (per serving): 455	
Protein (per serving): 49	
Fat (per serving): 19	
Nutritional value: ● ●	

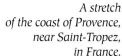

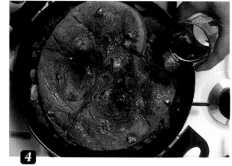

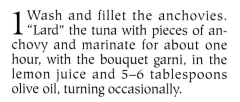

1 Wash and fillet the anchovies. "Lard" the tuna with pieces of anchovy and marinate for about one hour, with the bouquet garni, in the lemon juice and 5–6 tablespoons olive oil, turning occasionally.

2 Drain the tuna and reserve the marinade. Wash and dice the tomatoes. Peel the onion and mince; sauté over low heat until soft in the marinade oil.

3 Add the tomatoes and the crushed garlic and continue to simmer over low heat for about 15 minutes.

4 Add the tuna to the sauce and adjust salt and pepper. Add 1 cup white wine. Cover and cook over moderate heat for about 40 minutes. Serve the tuna smothered in its fragrant sauce.

A stretch of the coast of Provence, near Saint-Tropez, in France.

CHIPIRONES A LA MALAGUEÑA

Stuffed Squid

4 squid
   (800–900 g/1 ³/4 – 2 lbs
   total weight)
250 g/1 ¹/3 cups rice
500 g/1 lb mussels
¹/2 leek
1 onion
3 stalks celery
Tomato purée
Flour
Vegetable broth (see p. 44)
Dry white wine
90 g/6 tbsp butter
Olive oil

Servings:	4
Preparation time:	25'
Cooking time:	1h 30 + 30'
Difficulty:	●●●
Flavor:	●●
Kcal (per serving):	617
Protein (per serving):	32
Fat (per serving):	26
Nutritional value:	●●

1 Scrub the mussels; open and shell. Clean the squid, removing the beaks, eyes, and all entrails. Separate the bodies from the tentacles. Sauté the chopped leek until soft in 4–5 tablespoons olive oil. Add the chopped tentacles, salt, and pepper, and cook a few minutes longer. Add the mussel meats and ¹/2 cup wine; simmer for 10 minutes.

2 Gently sauté the minced onion in 2 tablespoons butter and 3–4 tablespoons olive oil; add and "toast"

the rice. Add about 1 cup tomato purée and the Step 1 ingredients; simmer until the rice is just tender, adding hot broth by the ladleful as needed.

3 Stuff the squid with the rice mixture. Align in a buttered baking dish; season with salt and pepper; add ¹/2 cup hot broth. Bake at 180°C/350°F for about 35 minutes, adding broth a little at a time as needed.

4 Blanch the celery and cut into pieces. Melt the remaining butter over very low heat. Stir in 4 tablespoons flour and then add 1 ¹/2 cups hot broth, a little at a time, while stirring. The bechamel should be rather liquid in consistency. Process in a food mixer with the celery. Serve the squid with the celery sauce on the side, garnished with sprigs of parsley.

TRIGLIE IN TEGLIA

Pan-Cooked Mullet

1 kg/2 1/2 lbs red rock mullets
4–5 ripe tomatoes
2 cloves garlic
Oregano
Parsley
Olive oil

Servings: 4	
Preparation time: 20'	
Cooking time: 20'	
Difficulty: ● ●	
Flavor: ● ●	
Kcal (per serving): 412	
Protein (per serving): 33	
Fat (per serving): 27	
Nutritional value: ● ●	

Rinse and clean the fish. Heat 3–4 tablespoons olive oil and 1 clove garlic over low heat. Remove the garlic before it begins to brown. Add the diced tomatoes and simmer for a few minutes; add the other garlic clove, minced with parsley, and salt and pepper. Cook over low heat for about 10 minutes, until the sauce is somewhat thickened. Lay the fish on the sauce base and cook for 6–7 minutes per side. Before serving, adjust salt and pepper and sprinkle the fish with oregano.

TRIGLIE ALLA LIVORNESE

Mullet Livorno Style

Rinse and clean the fish. Flour them on both sides and fry until golden in 5–6 tablespoons olive oil.
Remove the fish from the pan and drain on absorbent paper. Sauté the minced onion and garlic until golden in the same oil; add the crushed tomatoes and simmer for about 10 minutes. Lay the fish on the sauce base and continue cooking, adjusting salt and pepper if necessary and turning the fish occasionally (but very carefully, since they are extremely fragile), until the sauce is thickened.
Serve the fish hot in the sauce, dusted with minced parsley.

800 g/1 3/4 lbs medium
   red rock mullets
1/2 onion
2 cloves garlic
4–5 ripe tomatoes
Flour
Parsley
Olive oil

Servings:	4
Preparation time:	10′
Cooking time:	30′
Difficulty:	●
Flavor:	● ● ●
Kcal (per serving):	464
Protein (per serving):	34
Fat (per serving):	27
Nutritional value:	● ●

BARBOUNIA ME DOLMADAKIA

Mullets in Grape Leaves

18 medium mullets, cleaned and scaled
18 large grape leaves
Parsley, basil, oregano, mint, dill, thyme (minced together)
Juice and peel of 1 lemon
Capers
Olive oil

Servings: 6	
Preparation time: 15'	
Cooking time: 15'	
Difficulty: ● ●	
Flavor: ● ●	
Kcal (per serving): 377	
Protein (per serving): 2	
Fat (per serving): 32	
Nutritional value: ●	

Blanch the grape leaves for 4–5 minutes; drain and dry carefully. Season the cavity of the mullets with salt and pepper and place a small piece of lemon peel in each. Wrap each fish in a grape leaf, leaving the head and tail uncovered; tie with kitchen twine so that the leaf does not unroll during cooking. Grill for about 10 minutes. Prepare the vinaigrette. With a wire whisk or fork, beat the lemon juice (2–3 tablespoons) with 6–8 tablespoons extra virgin olive oil. Add salt, pepper, 4 tablespoons of the minced herbs and 1 tablespoon minced capers. Serve the fish as soon as it is tender, with the sauce on the side or poured over the fish on the serving platter.

ONE-DISH MEALS

5

COUSCOUS BIDAOUÏ

Couscous with Lamb

1 Cut the meat into stew-size pieces and place in a saucepan with a little less than 1 liter (4 cups) boiling water, a dash of salt and pepper, 1 chopped onion, the cabbage, cut into strips, and half the butter. Clean and peel the vegetables and the second onion and cut into chunks. Add to the meat along with the hot red pepper and a 1 teaspoon coriander. Cover and cook slowly for 45 minutes, then add the saffron.

2 In the meantime, rinse and drain the couscous. Place it into a bowl, add 1 tablespoon oil and a dash of salt; stir and set aside for 30 minutes.

3 Rub the couscous on the palm of your hand to form tiny balls; shake off excess grains in a strainer.

4 Steam the couscous in a couscoussière, or in a colander with small holes, over a pan of boiling water, add a pat of butter now and then and stir occasionally. Place the couscous on a serving platter, top with the meat mixture, and serve.

		Servings: 4
400 g/1 lb boned shoulder of lamb (or mutton)	200 g/1 1/2 lbs yellow squash	Preparation time: 10' + 30'
	1 hot red pepper	Cooking time: 45'
400 g/1 lb semolina for couscous	Coriander seeds	Difficulty: ● ● ●
2 carrots	Powdered saffron	Flavor: ● ●
2 tomatoes	100 g/1/2 cup butter	Kcal (per serving): 682
2 onions	Olive oil	Protein (per serving): 30
1/2 head cabbage		Fat (per serving): 39
1 eggplant		Nutritional value: ● ●

If you don't want to go to the trouble of preparing the couscous in the traditional manner (steps 2 and 3), use the quick-cooking parboiled couscous available at any supermarket.

MOUSSAKA

Eggplant au Gratin

1.5 kg/3 ¹/₂ lbs eggplant
750 g/1 ¹/₂ lbs ground beef
1 onion, parsley
3–4 peeled tomatoes
2 eggs
50 g/4 tbsp fine dry
   breadcrumbs
Parmesan cheese, grated
Red wine
Butter
Vegetable oil for frying

For the white sauce
¹/₂ liter milk
5 tbsp flour
6 tbsp butter

Servings: 6	
Preparation time: 15′ + 30′	
Cooking time: 2h 15′	
Difficulty:	● ● ●
Flavor:	● ●
Kcal (per serving): 848	
Protein (per serving): 25	
Fat (per serving): 30	
Nutritional value:	● ●

The village of Pylos in Greece's Peloponnese region.

1 Slice the eggplant, sprinkle the slices with salt and allow to stand, weighted, for ¹/₂ hour until the moisture is squeezed out. Melt about 3 tablespoons butter over low heat; add the minced onion and cook until soft; add the meat and 4 tablespoons water; mix well.

2 Add the diced tomatoes, 2 tablespoons minced parsley, 1 cup wine, and salt and pepper. Cover and simmer for 45 minutes. In the meantime, prepare the white sauce: over very low heat, blend the flour into the melted butter; add the warmed milk a little at a time, stirring constantly. When thickened, adjust salt and pepper to taste.

3 Remove the sauce from the heat and fold in the bread crumbs and the stiffly-beaten egg whites. When the sauce has cooled, fold in the beaten yolks and about ¹/₃ cup grated Parmesan cheese. In the meantime, rinse and dry the eggplant slices, and sauté in hot vegetable oil until golden. Drain well on absorbent paper.

4 Place a layer of eggplant slices in a buttered baking pan; cover with a layer of the meat sauce and another of white sauce. Continue

until the ingredients are used up, ending with a layer of eggplant. Dust with grated Parmesan cheese and bake in a preheated 180°C/350°F oven for about 45 minutes.

PAELLA

Rinse the peppers and place in a preheated 250°C/450–500°F oven for about 20 minutes or until the skin is darkened. Remove from the oven, skin, remove the stems, seeds, and white fibrous membranes; dice. Reduce the oven heat to 180°C/350°F. Blanch the tomatoes, skin, and chop. Peel the garlic and the onion and mince very finely. Dice the pork. Scrub and debeard the mussels; clean the scampi.

1 Heat ¼ cup or more olive oil in a paellero or a generous lidded casserole. Sauté the chicken pieces until golden; remove from the pan, drain, sprinkle with salt and pepper, and reserve.

2 Lightly sauté the pork in the oil left in the pan; add the mussels and the scampi. When the mussels open and the scampi have turned pink, remove the meats and shellfish from the pan.

3 Cook the garlic and onion until soft in the remaining oil. Add the tomatoes and peas and simmer for 5 minutes. In the meantime, heat 1 ¼ liters broth almost to boiling. To the contents of the paellero, add the saffron, ½ teaspoon Cayenne, salt, ground black pepper, and the bay leaf. Pour in the rice, and immediately thereafter the hot broth. Simmer over very low heat for 25 minutes, until the broth is completely absorbed by the rice. Add the sweet

peppers, mix well, and place the chicken, the pork, the scampi and the opened mussels (throw away those that do not open) on top.
Cover and bake on the center rack in a 180°C/350°F oven for 15 minutes or more. Serve the paella with lemon quarters on the side.

---

1 chicken, 1.2 kg/ca. 2 ½ lbs, cut into 12 pieces
250 g/½ lb lean pork
500 g/1 lb mussels
6 large scampi
2 sweet red peppers
500 g/2 ¾ cups rice for risotto
600g/1 ½ lbs tomatoes
1 onion
5 cloves garlic
300 g/1 cup shelled peas
1 envelope saffron
1 bay leaf
Chicken or beef broth
1 lemon
Cayenne pepper
Olive oil

Servings: 6	
Preparation time: 45'	
Cooking time: 1h 30'	
Difficulty: ● ● ●	
Flavor: ● ● ●	
Kcal (per serving): 928	
Protein (per serving): 49	
Fat (per serving): 41	
Nutritional value: ● ● ●	

MATISHA MAHSHEEYA

Stuffed Tomatoes

4 ripe tomatoes
350 g/2 cups long-grain rice
    (Basmati)
1 onion
1 carrot
Parsley
4–6 radishes
Hot red pepper, ground
Cayenne pepper
1 lemon
Vegetable broth (see p. 44)
Olive oil

Servings: 4	
Preparation time: 40'+2-3h	
Cooking time: 40'	
Difficulty: ● ●	
Flavor: ● ●	
Kcal (per serving): 523	
Protein (per serving): 8	
Fat (per serving): 16	
Nutritional value: ●	

Vegetable broth (see p. 44)

1 Wash the tomatoes. Cut off the "lids" and set aside; scoop out the insides, and salt the shells lightly.

2 Gently sauté the sliced onion and the carrot (cut into cubes), in a skillet with 4-5 tablespoons olive oil for about 30 minutes.

3 Boil the rice in the vegetable broth (20 minutes), drain, add a squiggle of olive oil, and set aside to cool.

4 Slice the radishes thinly and add to the rice with the sautéed carrot and onion, a sprig of chopped parsley, the grated rind and juice of the lemon, and a pinch each of salt, Cayenne pepper, and ground hot red pepper. Fill the tomatoes with the rice mixture and replace the "lids". Refrigerate for 2-3 hours before serving.

146

İÇLI TAVA

Rice with Anchovies

240 g/1 1/3 cups rice
1 kg/2 1/4 lbs fresh anchovies
1 onion
Raisins
Cinnamon
Sugar
70 g/5 tbsp butter
Olive oil

Servings: 4	
Preparation time: 50'	
Cooking time: 35' + 1h	
Difficulty:	● ●
Flavor:	● ●
Kcal (per serving):	740
Protein (per serving):	38
Fat (per serving):	36
Nutritional value:	● ●

1 Chop the onion finely and sauté in a skillet in 2 tablespoons olive oil. Add a handful of raisins, 1 teaspoon sugar, a tiny pinch of ground cinnamon, salt and pepper.

2 Add the rice and toast over a lively flame for 1 minute; add a ladle of boiling water; lower the flame and cook the rice for 20 minutes, adding boiling water as needed. Turn off the flame and blend in a pat of butter.

The busy ferry port of Istanbul (Turkey) on the Bosphorus.

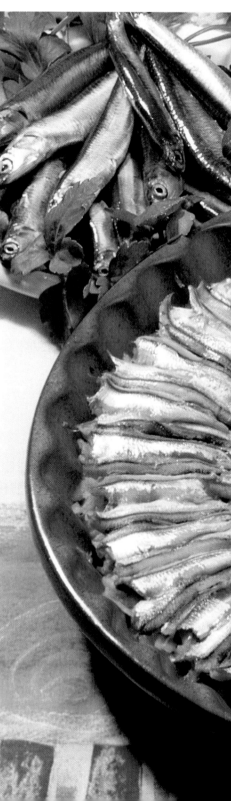

3 Clean and wash the anchovies, removing the heads and bones; arrange half the anchovies in a spoke pattern in a greased baking dish.

4 Cover the fish with the rice, smooth it down, and make another layer of anchovies with the tails toward the center. Dot with the rest of the butter and bake at 180°C/350°F for 15 minutes.

ZARZUELA

1 Northern lobster or 1 spiny
  lobster, 1 kg/2–2 ¹/₂ lbs,
  boiled
18 scallops
12 scampi
12 large mussels
24 clams
1 cup Xères (sherry)
1 cup dry white wine
Juice of 1 lemon
400 g/1 lb onions
2 cloves garlic
2 sweet peppers (1 red,
  1 green)
1 kg/2 ¹/₄ lbs tomatoes
100 g/¹/₄ lb almonds
100 g/¹/₄ lb prosciutto ham
2 envelopes saffron
1 bouquet garni (parsley,
  thyme, bay leaf)
1 bunch parsley, minced
Olive oil

Servings: 6	
Preparation time: 45'	
Cooking time: 1h 15'	
Difficulty:	●●
Flavor:	●●
Kcal (per serving): 684	
Protein (per serving): 39	
Fat (per serving): 35	
Nutritional value:	●●

1 Peel and mince the onions and garlic. Remove the stems, seeds, and white fibrous membranes from the peppers; dice.
Heat a few tablespoons olive oil in a large pan (better yet, a paellero). Add the minced garlic and onion and the peppers; cook over low heat so that the ingredients do not darken.

2 Meanwhile, dip the tomatoes in boiling water; skin and trim. Chop finely. Cut the prosciutto into thin strips. Scrub and de-beard the mussels. Scrub the scallops. Soak the clams, changing the water frequently. Sauté the scampi in 2 tablespoons olive oil for 5 minutes. Pick over the lobster, extracting all the meat.

3 To the ingredients in the pan, add the tomatoes, the wine, the Xères, the lemon juice, the bouquet garni, and the finely-chopped almonds. Add salt and pepper and cook over high heat for about 5 minutes.

4 Add the saffron diluted in 2 tablespoons water, the clams, the mussels, the cleaned and rinsed scallops, the lobster meat, and the scampi. Turn down the heat, mix well, cover, and simmer for about 10 minutes, the time needed to open the mollusks. Just before serving, remove the bouquet garni and sprinkle with minced parsley. Serve very hot.

FOCACCIA ALLA PROVOLA

Provola Pie

Focaccia dough (see p. 154)	
200 g/¹/₂ lb fresh green beans	
200 g/¹/₂ lb smoked provola cheese	
100 g/4 oz dried mushrooms	
300 g/³/₄ lb ripe tomatoes	
Parsley	
Olive oil	

Servings: 6	
Preparation time: 35' + 1h	
Cooking time: 40'	
Difficulty: ● ● ●	
Flavor: ● ● ●	
Kcal (per serving): 643	
Protein (per serving): 21	
Fat (per serving): 31	
Nutritional value: ● ●	

1 Prepare the dough; while it is rising, soak the mushrooms in warm water. Trim the beans, blanch in lightly salted boiling water, drain, and cut into 1-inch lengths.

2 Squeeze the mushrooms to remove excess moisture; sauté lightly in 3–4 tablespoons olive oil with a pinch of salt; add the diced tomatoes.

3 Simmer for 7–8 minutes. Add the green beans, salt, and pepper and simmer for 5–6 minutes longer. Remove from the heat.

4 Mix in the diced provola cheese and a tablespoon or two minced parsley. Roll out the dough into two rounds, one larger and one smaller. Cut "windows" (with a triangular or other cutter) in the smaller disk of dough. Grease a round baking pan with removable rim and line with the larger disk of dough. Do not trim the excess. Pour in the filling. Lay the smaller disk of dough on top and fold up the edges of the first disk to form a uniform border. Brush the top with olive oil and bake in a preheated 200°C/375–400°F oven for 20 minutes.

FOCACCIA MEZZOGIORNO

Eggplant and Pepper Pie

Focaccia dough (made with
  whole wheat flour, if desired)
1 eggplant
4 sweet peppers, yellow and red
1 white onion
200 g/^{1}/$_2$ lb goat-milk ricotta
  cheese
2 eggs
Parmesan cheese, grated
1 sprig mint
Olive oil

Servings:6	
Preparation time: 35' + 1h	
Cooking time: 50'	
Difficulty: ● ● ●	
Flavor: ● ● ●	
Kcal (per serving): 580	
Protein (per serving): 19	
Fat (per serving): 29	
Nutritional value: ●	

Focaccia dough

*Dissolve ^{2}/$_3$ oz (1 cake)
compressed yeast in warm
water. Make a well with
3 ^{3}/$_4$ cups flour, pour the
yeast mixture into the center
with 1 tablespoon olive oil
and a pinch of salt. Work
the flour into the liquid,
adding more water if
required. Form into a ball
and allow to rise for one
hour. Roll out to the desired
thickness with a floured
rolling pin.*

1 Prepare the dough and set aside to rise. Wash the eggplant and the peppers. Remove the stems, seeds, and white fibrous membranes from the peppers and cut into lengthwise strips. Dice the eggplant, sprinkle with salt, and allow to drip on a rack.

2 Sauté the sliced onion in 3–4 tablespoons olive oil until soft. When it begins to color, add the peppers and salt and pepper; cover and simmer for about 10 minutes.

3 Rinse and dry the eggplant; add to the pan and continue cooking for another 10 minutes, adding water if necessary.

4 Beat the eggs with the ricotta cheese, 2 tablespoons Parmesan, and salt and pepper to taste, until light and well-blended. Blend in the cooled pepper-and-eggplant mixture and the mint.
Roll the dough out into two rounds, one larger and one smaller. Grease a round baking pan with removable rim and line with the larger disk of dough. Pour in the filling. Cover with the smaller disk of dough and seal the edges. Use the leftover dough to create a floral design on the top crust. Brush the surface with olive oil, pierce with a fork, and bake in a preheated 200°C/375–400°F oven for about 30 minutes. Serve warm or cold.

SPANAKOPITA

Greek Spinach Pie

5 disks frozen puff paste
1 kg/2 ¼ lbs fresh spinach
200 g/½ lb green onions
Parsley
Dill
150 g/5–6 oz Greek feta cheese
50 g/3–4 tbsp butter
Milk
2 eggs + 1 yolk
Ground anise
Olive oil

Servings: 6	
Preparation time: 30'	
Cooking time: 1h	
Difficulty: ● ●	
Flavor: ● ●	
Kcal (per serving): 1138	
Protein (per serving): 87	
Fat (per serving): 37	
Nutritional value: ● ● ●	

Wash the spinach repeatedly to remove all sand and soil. Eliminate the stems and the toughest ribs. Shake dry; cook for about 10 minutes, preferably without adding more water. When cool enough to handle, squeeze to remove excess liquid. Mince and reserve.

1 Sauté the sliced green onions in olive oil until transparent, then add the spinach and cook for about 10 minutes. Allow to cool. While still slightly warm, add a few tablespoons chopped parsley and dill, the two whole eggs, the crumbled cheese, salt and pepper to taste, and a pinch of ground anise. Mix well.

2 Butter a round pan with a removable rim and place 3 disks of puff paste in the bottom. Heat 3/4 cup milk; remove from the heat and add the rest of the butter. When melted, brush over the puff paste. Lay another disk on top and again brush with the milk mixture. Pour in the spinach filling and cover with the last disk of puff paste. Brush with the milk mixture. With the point of a knife, trace parallel and perpendicular lines to form a diamond pattern. To the remaining milk mixture, add 1 egg yolk beaten with a few drops water. Pour over the top of the pie. Bake at 200°C/375–400°F for 40 minutes. Cool for a few minutes before making a small cut in the crust to allow the steam to escape.

VEGETABLES, SALADS, AND EGG DISHES

6

ARTICHAUTS À LA BARIGOULE

Artichokes "à la Barigoule"

8 *violetto* artichokes
1 onion
1 carrot
2 cloves garlic
Parsley
2 slices day-old bakery bread
    with crusts removed
Dry white wine
Olive oil

Servings: 4	
Preparation time: 25′	
Cooking time: 1h 30′	
Difficulty: ● ●	
Flavor: ● ●	
Kcal (per serving): 369	
Protein (per serving): 11	
Fat (per serving): 10	
Nutritional value: ● ●	

Trim the artichokes; cut off the stem and the tops of the leaves; turn upside down and press on a flat surface to open the leaves a bit. Mince the garlic with parsley; mix with the crumbled bread. Peel the onion and the carrot; mince finely and place in the bottom of a deep baking pan with 4 tablespoons olive oil. Set the artichokes in the pan, right side up. Place some of the breadcrumb mixture on each artichoke, pressing a little to work it down between the leaves. Drizzle each artichoke with olive oil; salt and pepper. Pour 1 cup wine over the artichokes. Bake, covered, in a slow (140°C/300°F) oven for 1 1/2 hours.

LARDISHAWKI MAHSHI

Stuffed Artichokes

1 Trim the artichokes; remove the stems, the tough outer leaves, and the tops of the remaining leaves. Sauté in 3–4 tablespoons olive oil; drain and reserve. In the same oil, sauté the ground beef with the finely-chopped onion, the pine nuts, a pinch of salt, and 1/4 teaspoon cinnamon.

2 Fill each artichoke with a tablespoon or more of the meat mixture. Place upright in an oiled baking pan. Pour in enough hot water to cover the artichokes halfway. Bake at 140°C/300°F for about 45 minutes.

10–12 artichokes
600 g/1 1/2 lbs ground beef
2 onions
50 g/1/4 cup pine nuts
Ground cinnamon
Olive oil

Servings:	4
Preparation time:	20'
Cooking time:	1h
Difficulty:	● ●
Flavor:	● ●
Kcal (per serving):	418
Protein (per serving):	40
Fat (per serving):	19
Nutritional value:	● ●

SALADE NIÇOISE

Riviera Salad

1 head lettuce
150 g/6 oz tuna in olive oil
4 ripe tomatoes
1 sweet pepper
1 stalk celery, with leaves
2 artichokes
2 green onions
4 eggs
4 anchovies
12 black olives
Juice of 1 lemon
Vinegar
Olive oil

Servings: 4

Preparation time: 20'

Cooking time: 12'

Difficulty: ●

Flavor: ● ●

Kcal (per serving): 492

Protein (per serving): 33

Fat (per serving): 32

Nutritional value: ● ● ●

Open the anchovies, remove the entrails and bones, rinse well and fillet. Wash the artichokes, remove the stems, the tough outer leaves, and the tops; blanch in lightly salted water with lemon juice added; drain. Hard-boil the eggs (7 minutes), shell, and cut into wedges.

Wash the peppers and the tomatoes; trim and seed both. Cut the peppers lengthwise into strips and the tomatoes into wedges.

Trim and rinse the lettuce and the green onions; cut the latter into thin rounds. Wash the celery and slice crosswise.

In a salad bowl, form a layer of half the lettuce, tomatoes, artichokes (sliced crosswise), peppers, tuna (drained and crumbled), celery, and onions. Make another layer in the same manner with the other half of the same ingredients. Top with the olives, anchovies, and egg wedges.

Shake or beat 1 tablespoon vinegar with 6 tablespoons olive oil and a pinch of salt and pepper. Pour over this classic, fragrant salad and serve with fresh crusty bread.

INSALATA DI ARANCE

Orange Salad

Peel the oranges and remove all the white inner skin. Separate the sections, remove the membrane from each, and cut into pieces. Arrange the pieces of orange on a bed of lettuce and sprinkle with chopped parsley. Dress the salad with a little olive oil, salt, and freshly-ground pepper. This is a fresh and delicious accompaniment to roast meats.

6 oranges (preferably *tarocco*, not overly ripe)
2–3 sprigs parsley
Olive oil

Servings:	4
Preparation time:	15'
Difficulty:	●
Flavor:	●
Kcal (per serving):	210
Protein (per serving):	2
Fat (per serving):	15
Nutritional value:	● ● ●

TABBULEH

Bulghur Salad

120 g/4 oz precooked bulghur
3 tomatoes
1 onion
250 g/1/2 lb parsley
2 lemons
Fresh mint
Tender lettuce leaves
   (as garnish)
Olive oil

Servings: 4	
Preparation time: 15' + 1h 20'	
Difficulty: ●	
Flavor: ●●	
Kcal (per serving): 234	
Protein (per serving): 5	
Fat (per serving): 11	
Nutritional value: ●●	

1 Soak the bulghur in 1 1/2 cups water for 20 minutes or according to package directions; drain and transfer to a large bowl. Beat the juice of 1 lemon with 4 tablespoons olive oil, salt, and pepper, and pour over the cereal. Mix well and allow to stand for about 1 hour. Wash and dry the parsley and mint. Eliminate the stems and mince the leaves. Set aside. Peel and mince the onion and mix into the bulghur.

2 Add the minced herbs to the bulghur and mix well; add the juice of the second lemon blended with 4 tablespoons olive oil and toss until well coated.

Bulghur is a parched, cracked wheat, cooked by steaming. You can find this product in gourmet food and herbalist's shops – and more and more often in the supermarkets.

3 Add the cleaned and diced tomatoes. Mix again. Transfer to a serving bowl lined with lettuce leaves; garnish as desired. This is a rich and tasty dish all by itself, but is also an excellent side with timbales, soufflés, savory pies, etc.

Michoteta

Cheese Salad

350 g/³/₄ lb soft fresh cheese
   (crescenza) or very thick
   yoghurt
1 onion
1 cucumber
Juice of 2 lemons
Olive oil

Servings: 4	
Preparation time: 20' + 30'	
Difficulty: ● ●	
Flavor: ● ●	
Kcal (per serving): 368	
Protein (per serving): 17	
Fat (per serving): 31	
Nutritional value: ● ● ●	

In a bowl, soften the cheese with a fork
until creamy. Dress with the lemon juice
blended with 6–8 tablespoons olive oil and
allow to stand for 30 minutes. Peel the onion
and chop finely; dice the cucumber. Fold these
ingredients into the cheese, season with salt and
pepper to taste, and mix again gently.
This salad is excellent served with Greek pita bread or
with the Italian *piadina*, two typical Mediterranean flat
loaves.

Meshouïa o Mechouïa

Tuna and Pepper Salad

Boil the eggs for 7 minutes; shell and chop coarsely. Roast the peppers in the oven; when cool enough to handle, skin and remove the stems, seeds, and membranes; cut into strips. Clean the tomatoes and cut into wedges. Mince the onion and garlic together and place in a salad bowl with the cumin ground in a mortar with a pinch of salt, the peppers, the tomatoes, the eggs, the broken-up olives, and the drained and crumbled tuna.

For the dressing, whip or shake the lemon juice with 8 tablespoons olive oil. Toss the salad and serve.

200 g/8 oz tuna packed in oil
2 sweet peppers
2 tomatoes
2 eggs
1 onion
1 clove garlic
12 black olives, pitted
Juice of 1 lemon
1 tsp cumin seeds
Olive oil

Servings: 4	
Preparation time: 30′ + 30′	
Difficulty: ● ●	
Flavor: ● ●	
Kcal (per serving): 366	
Protein (per serving): 22	
Fat (per serving): 28	
Nutritional value: ● ● ●	

MELANZANE RIPIENE

Stuffed Eggplant

4–5 eggplants (8 if small)
1 onion
50 g/2 oz salami
2 egg whites
2 cloves garlic
2–3 anchovies packed in salt
Capers packed in salt
Fine dry breadcrumbs
Parsley
Olive oil
Vegetable oil for frying

Servings: 4	
Preparation time: 45′	
Cooking time: 30′	
Difficulty: ● ● ●	
Flavor: ● ● ●	
Kcal (per serving): 500	
Protein (per serving): 14	
Fat (per serving): 42	
Nutritional value: ● ● ●	

1 Trim the eggplant and cut in half lengthwise. Blanch in salted water and drain while still very firm. Remove the pulp, taking care not to break the shells, and reserve. Toast $^1/_4$ to $^1/_3$ cup breadcrumbs in a frying pan.

2 Cut the onion into thin lengthwise slices; sauté in 3–4 tablespoons olive oil until soft. Add the eggplant pulp and a pinch of salt and simmer for a few minutes.

3 Add the rinsed capers, the thoroughly rinsed and filleted anchovies, the garlic minced with parsley, and the diced salami. Mix and simmer for a few minutes to allow the flavors to blend; add the breadcrumbs and remove from the heat.

4 Stuff the eggplant shells with the mixture, sealing with more breadcrumbs mixed with beaten egg white. Fry in deep hot oil, first upside-down (on the filling side) and then on the other sides.

PEPERONI RIPIENI

Stuffed Peppers

3 Remove the "hat" from the peppers and eliminate the seeds and white fibrous membranes without breaking the shells. Fill to the brim with the filling mixture.

4 Dip the open end in the beaten egg and then in breadcrumbs. Fry in deep hot oil, first upside-down (on the filling side) and then – when a golden crust has formed on the top – lower the heat and fry on the other sides.

1 Cut the onion into thin lengthwise slices and sauté lightly with the minced parsley in 4–5 tablespoons olive oil for 4–5 minutes. Remove from the heat and add enough breadcrumbs to absorb all the oil.

2 When the mixture has cooled, mix in the grated pecorino cheese, the garlic minced with 2–3 tablespoons parsley, and the washed and diced anchovies. If the mixture seems too compact, add a few drops water. Adjust the salt and pepper.

4 sweet peppers
1 onion
1 clove garlic
2–3 anchovies packed in salt
1 egg
100 g/1/4 lb pecorino cheese
   with peppercorns, grated
Parsley
Fine dry breadcrumbs

Olive oil
Vegetable oil for frying

Servings: 4	
Preparation time: 40'	
Cooking time: 20'	
Difficulty: ● ● ●	
Flavor: ● ● ●	
Kcal (per serving): 518	
Protein (per serving): 15	
Fat (per serving): 45	
Nutritional value: ● ● ●	

RATATOUILLE

2 onions
2 sweet peppers
2 zucchini
5 ripe tomatoes
4–5 cloves garlic
1 eggplant
1 bouquet garni (bay leaf, basil, parsley, wild fennel, thyme)
Olive oil

Servings: 4	
Preparation time: 25' + 30'	
Cooking time: 30'	
Difficulty: ● ●	
Flavor: ● ● ●	
Kcal (per serving): 156	
Protein (per serving): 3	
Fat (per serving): 10	
Nutritional value: ● ●	

Skin the eggplant and cut into slices. Sprinkle the slices with coarse salt and allow to stand, weighted, for $1/2$ hour until the moisture is squeezed out.

Peel and slice the onion. Rinse the tomatoes, open them lengthwise, seed, and dice. Rinse and trim the zucchini; dice without peeling. Rinse the peppers; remove the stems, seeds, and white fibrous membranes and cut into thin lengthwise strips. Drain the eggplant, rinse, dry, and dice. When all the vegetables are ready, place them in a wide, deep pan with the bouquet garni, the garlic, and 2 tablespoons olive oil. Simmer for $1/2$ hour; adjust salt and pepper.

The classic ratatouille, a traditional mixed vegetable dish, is excellent either hot or cold, all by itself (served with couscous or bulghur, or with bread) or as a side dish with meats and fish.

Zucchine Fritte

Fried Zucchini

Lightly toast about ¹/₂ cup breadcrumbs in a non-stick frying pan. Rinse and trim the zucchini, slice lengthwise, and sauté until golden in 4–5 tablespoons olive oil with the whole garlic clove. Eliminate the garlic. Place a layer of zucchini in an oven-proof dish. Sprinkle with breadcrumbs, a few leaves of tarragon, mint, and oregano, and salt and pepper. Place a second layer of zucchini on top; sprinkle with breadcrumbs and herbs; repeat until all the ingredients are used up.
Drizzle a few tablespoons olive oil over the top and sprinkle with vinegar and crushed hot red pepper. Bake in a preheated 200°C/375–400°F oven for 10 minutes. Excellent served hot, but also delicious cold.

4–5 zucchini
1 clove garlic
Fine dry breadcrumbs
Fresh tarragon
Fresh mint
Fresh oregano
1 hot red pepper
Vinegar
Olive oil

Servings: 4	
Preparation time: 30'	
Cooking time: 20'	
Difficulty: ●●	
Flavor: ●●	
Kcal (per serving): 163	
Protein (per serving): 3	
Fat (per serving): 10	
Nutritional value: ●●●	

FRITTATA AL BASILICO

Basil Omelette

4–5 eggs
Fine dry breadcrumbs
Basil
Grated pecorino cheese
Olive oil

Servings: 4	
Preparation time: 10'	
Cooking time: 10'	
Difficulty: ●	
Flavor: ●	
Kcal (per serving): 437	
Protein (per serving): 20	
Fat (per serving): 33	
Nutritional value: ● ●	

Beat the eggs with a whisk, adding a pinch of salt and pepper, $^1/_4$ to $^1/_2$ cup grated pecorino cheese, 1 tablespoon breadcrumbs, and a large handful of basil leaves.

Cook the omelette in a very hot, lightly oiled pan (preferable cast iron) until it sets; turn, and serve immediately.

OMELETTE À LA PROVENÇALE

Omelette Provençal

4 eggs
1 green onion
2 ripe tomatoes
2 cloves garlic
Basil
Parsley
1 white onion or 1 leek, and
    1 tomato (as garnish)
Olive oil

Servings: 4
Preparation time: 20'
Cooking time: 20'
Difficulty: ● ●
Flavor: ● ●
Kcal (per serving): 292
Protein (per serving): 11
Fat (per serving): 25
Nutritional value: ●

Wash and seed the tomatoes; dice. Trim the green onion, cut it into thin rounds, and sauté until soft with 4–5 tablespoons olive oil. Add the tomatoes, the peeled, crushed garlic, and salt and pepper to taste.

Cook over very low heat for about 15 minutes, then add the eggs beaten with 2–3 tablespoons parsley and basil, minced together. As soon as the omelette sets, turn it with the aid of a plate and complete cooking over low heat; adjust salt and pepper. Serve garnished with rounds of ripe tomato and onion or leek rings.

4 eggs
250 g/¹/₂ lb fresh anchovies
Flour
Parsley
Tomatoes and lettuce
  (for garnish)
Olive oil

Servings: 4	
Preparation time: 30′	
Cooking time: 30′	
Difficulty: ● ●	
Flavor: ● ●	
Kcal (per serving): 347	
Protein (per serving): 24	
Fat (per serving): 20	
Nutritional value: ● ●	

HAMSI KAYGANASI

Anchovy Omelette

Gut the anchovies and remove the bones, heads, and tails. Beat the eggs with 1 tablespoon flour and a pinch of salt. Add the broken-up anchovies and a sprig of chopped parsley. Heat 2–3 tablespoons olive oil in a pan, pour in the egg mixture, lower the flame, cover and cook slowly for about 5 minutes. Use the lid or a plate to turn the omelet and cook the other side for 5 minutes as well. Serve garnished with lettuce and tomato.

OMELETTE ÉPICÉE

Spice Omelette

Peel the onions and stud with 2–3 cloves garlic each. Allow to stand for 4 hours in a pan of water to which you have added 1 cup vinegar, then boil in the same water for 2–3 minutes; drain. Cut the onions lengthwise into thin slices and sauté in 3–4 tablespoons olive oil. Pour in the eggs, beaten with a pinch of salt and pepper. When the omelette begins to set, turn with the aid of a plate and complete cooking.

*This omelette is excellent cold, garnished
with slices of ripe tomato and onion rings.*

4 eggs
3 onions
Whole cloves
1 onion and 1 tomato (as
    garnish)
White wine vinegar
Olive oil

Servings: 4	
Preparation time: 15' + 4h	
Cooking time: 20'	
Difficulty: ● ●	
Flavor: ● ●	
Kcal (per serving): 251	
Protein (per serving): 11	
Fat (per serving): 20	
Nutritional value: ●	

ODJA BIL GOMBRA

Scrambled Eggs with Shrimp

16 shrimp (crevettes)
4 eggs
2 tomatoes
2 fresh hot green peppers
2 cloves garlic
Parsley
Olive oil

Servings: 4	
Preparation time: 15'	
Cooking time: 30'	
Difficulty: ●	
Flavor: ● ●	
Kcal (per serving): 345	
Protein (per serving): 33	
Fat (per serving): 20	
Nutritional value: ● ●	

1 Rinse and dice the tomatoes; clean the peppers (eliminate the stems, seeds, and inner membranes) and dice. Sauté both vegetables lightly in 4 tablespoons olive oil, adding the finely minced garlic, salt, and pepper.

2 While the tomatoes are cooking, parboil the shrimp in lightly salted water. Shell and remove the heads, the carapace, and the black vein. Add the tails to the tomato mixture and simmer for 5 minutes over low heat. Break the eggs into the pan and stir rapidly to "scramble" them. Add salt if necessary. Serve immediately, sprinkled with a tablespoon or so of minced parsley.

DESSERTS

7

BABÀ

Baba au Rhum

For the baba
350 g/3 cups + 1 tbsp flour
60 g/5 tbsp sugar
200 g/1 cup butter
30 g/1 oz compressed yeast
Milk
2 eggs

For the syrup
100 g/¹/₂ cup sugar
Rind of 1 lemon
1 cup rum

Servings: 4	
Preparation time: 30' + 1h	
Cooking time: 40'	
Difficulty: ● ●	
Kcal (per serving): 1615	
Protein (per serving): 16	
Fat (per serving): 49	
Nutritional value: ● ● ●	

Dissolve the yeast in 1 cup warm milk and mix into ¹/₃ of the flour to obtain a soft, smooth dough. Form into a ball and allow to rise to almost double its volume.

In the meantime, beat the eggs, cream the butter, and grease a deep fluted tube pan with more butter.

Make a well of the remaining flour on a working surface and work in all the ingredients listed for the baba, including the risen dough. Knead long and gently. Place the dough in the greased pan (only to one-third its depth). Cover and allow to rise.

When the dough has risen to ²/₃ the depth of the pan, begin baking in a warm oven (150°C/250–300°F) to ensure it cooks in the center. When it has risen to fill the mold, raise the heat to 190°C/375°F and continue baking until well-browned. Total baking time will be about 40 minutes.

Allow the cake to cool in the pan; remove carefully only when it is completely cooled.

While the cake is baking, prepare the syrup. Boil 2 cups water with the sugar and the lemon rind until syrupy (10 minutes or more). Cool slightly. Add the rum and mix well. Pour the syrup very slowly over the baba, using as much as the cake will absorb.

For a party look, decorate with whipped cream and candied fruit.

CANNOLI

To make cannoli, you will need the special tube molds for shaping the dough (at least two per serving).

150 g/1 1/3 cups flour
15 g/2 tbsp unsweetened cocoa
1 egg
25 g/2 tbsp sugar
1/2 cup Marsala wine
1 pinch salt
40 g/3 tbsp butter
Olive oil

For the filling
500 g/1 lb ricotta cheese
250 g/2 cups confectioners sugar
80 g/3 oz candied squash
100 g/4 oz semisweet
   chocolate (or semisweet
   chocolate chips)
Milk
Ground cinnamon
Candied orange peel

Servings: 6	
Preparation time: 25' + 1h	
Cooking time: 15'	
Difficulty: ● ●	
Kcal (per serving): 1221	
Protein (per serving): 17	
Fat (per serving): 72	
Nutritional value: ● ● ●	

On a working surface, combine the flour, egg, butter, sugar, the cocoa dissolved in the Marsala wine, and the salt. When the dough is smooth, form into a ball and allow to rest for about 1 hour. Roll out into a thin sheet. Cut into squares about 4 inches per side and roll up diagonally on the cannoli molds. Seal the top corners by dampening and pressing lightly with your finger.
Heat about 1 inch olive oil in a deep frying pan. When hot but not smoking, immerse the tubes with the cannoli; when golden brown, remove from the oil, drain, and allow to cool. In the meantime cream the ricotta with the confectioners sugar and a 1/4 teaspoon cinnamon. Use a wooden spatula to mix in a few drops milk.
The resulting cream should be smooth and fairly dense. Add the broken-up chocolate and the diced candied squash and mix.
Slide the fried cannoli off the molds; using a teaspoon, fill them with the cream.
Decorate with exposed surface of the cream with pieces of candied orange peel. Dust the tops of the cannoli with a little confectioners sugar and serve immediately.

CASSATA

3 Spoon the ricotta cream filling into the lined mold; level the top. Chill the cassata in the coldest part of the refrigerator for 2 hours or more (do not freeze).

4 Unmold the cassata on a serving platter. Spread with the pistachio icing and decorate with diced candied fruit, strips of candied squash, candied orange peel, sprinkles, etc.

1 Cream the ricotta in a bowl; add the confectioners sugar, 1/4 teaspoon vanilla extract, and 1/3 cup rum. Mix in the broken-up chocolate and 2 tablespoons diced candied fruit.

2 Line a round or rectangular mold with paper and line again with slices of sponge cake. Use a little of the ricotta cream to "glue" the vertical pieces.

Pistachio Icing

Beat 3–4 egg whites with 60 g (1 1/2–1 3/4 cups) confectioners sugar until stiff. Add enough lemon juice to obtain a good spreading consistency (the icing will harden later), a few drops green pistachio flavoring, and mix well.

150 g/6 oz flat sponge cake
450 g/1 lb ricotta cheese
120 g/1 cup confectioners sugar
50 g/2 oz semisweet chocolate
50 g/2 oz candied orange peel
Vanilla extract
Rum

Pistachio glaze (see facing page)
Candied fruit, squash, and orange peel
Silver sugar balls (and/or other edible decorations: sprinkles, chopped nuts, etc.)

Servings: 4	
Preparation time: 40' + 2h	
Difficulty: ●●	
Kcal (per serving): 916	
Protein (per serving): 23	
Fat (per serving): 24	
Nutritional value: ●●●	

Short pastry (recipe below)
Confectioners sugar

For the crème patissière
75 g/¹/₂ cup flour
3 egg yolks
3 tbsp sugar
2 cups milk
Grated rind of 1 lemon

For the filling
200 g/¹/₂ lb ricotta cheese
2 eggs
120 g/¹/₂ cup + 1 tbsp sugar
Millefiori essence
80 g/3 oz candied citron and
    orange peel

For the grain
150 g/6 oz wheat grains,
    soaked
1 cup milk
1 tbsp butter
¹/₄ tsp vanilla extract

Servings:	4
Preparation time:	30′ + 30′
Cooking time:	1h 30′ + 4h
Difficulty:	●●●
Kcal (per serving):	1354
Protein (per serving):	46
Fat (per serving):	55
Nutritional value:	●●●

Short Pastry
*Cream 125 g (¹/₂ cup)
butter and blend in
125 g (¹/₃ cup) sugar, a
pinch of salt, ¹/₄ teaspoon
vanilla extract, 2 egg yolks,
and 250 g (2 cups) flour.
Allow to stand for ¹/₂ hour
before using.*

PASTIERA NAPOLETANA

Neapolitan Easter Cake

The day before making the *pastiera*, simmer the wheat for 4 hours in the milk flavored with the vanilla. Add the butter. The wheat is cooked when the single grains open and the whole has reached a creamy consistency. Prepare the short pastry. Prepare the crème patissière: mix all the ingredients and cook over moderate heat for a few minutes; allow to cool. In a bowl, cream the ricotta with the sugar; add the crème patissière a little at a time, mixing gently, and the beaten egg yolks one at a time. Continue mixing, and add the cooled grain, the diced candied fruit, the millefiori essence, and the egg whites beaten to a stiff peak.

Spread half the pastry on a sheet of waxed paper in a disk of sufficient size to line a 25 cm diameter (10 inches) round pan, 4 cm (2 inches) deep. Butter the pan; invert the waxed paper over it and pat the pastry to line the pan. Pour in the ricotta mixture; level.

Spread the remaining pastry on another sheet of waxed paper. Cut strips about 2 cm (1 inch) wide and form a lattice over the top of the *pastiera*. Bake in a preheated 180°C/375–400°F oven for about 1 hour, or until the crust is golden brown. Cool and dust with confectioners sugar before serving.

RAVIOLI DOLCI

Sweet Ravioli

Mix the flour and $^1/_2$ cup water, the sugar, the lard, the beaten egg yolk, and $^1/_4$ teaspoon vanilla extract. Knead the dough until it is smooth and elastic; form into a ball and allow to rest for about $^1/_2$ hour.

To make the filling, cream the ricotta and work in the sugar, the lemon rind, $^1/_4$ teaspoon vanilla extract, a pinch of cinnamon, 1 tablespoon diced candied squash, and the broken-up chocolate. Mix thoroughly.

Roll out the pasta into a rather thin sheet and cut into squares about 15 cm (6 inches) per side.

Place a tablespoon or more of filling on one side of each square; fold the other half over the top and seal the ravioli with the cutter for that purpose.

Fry the ravioli in deep, very hot but not smoking oil; when they are golden brown, remove, drain, and dust with confectioners sugar.

For the dough
500 g/4 $^1/_4$ cups flour
100 g/$^1/_2$ cup + 1 tbsp sugar
80 g/3 oz lard (or butter)
1 egg yolk
Vanilla extract
Confectioners sugar
Vegetable oil for frying

For the filling
450 g/1 lb fresh ricotta cheese
120 g/$^1/_2$ cup + 1 tbsp sugar
Vanilla extract
Grated rind of $^1/_2$ lemon
Ground cinnamon
Candied squash
1 oz semisweet chocolate

Servings: 4
Preparation time: 1h + 30'
Cooking time: 30'
Difficulty: ● ●
Kcal (per serving): 1790
Protein (per serving): 27
Fat (per serving): 104
Nutritional value: ● ● ●

MAKROUD

Fried Date Cakes

250 g/8 oz semolina
100 g/4 oz fresh dates
100 g/4 oz sugar
Ground cinnamon
Salt
Olive oil
Vegetable oil

For the syrup
200 g/8 oz sugar
1 lemon

Servings: 4	
Preparation time: 50' + 45'	
Cooking time: 30'	
Difficulty: ● ● ●	
Kcal (per serving): 894	
Protein (per serving): 7	
Fat (per serving): 36	
Nutritional value: ● ● ●	

1 In a bowl, combine the semolina with 5 tablespoons olive oil and a pinch of salt. Add, a little at a time, enough lukewarm water to make a heavy dough. Allow to stand for 15 minutes. Knead well, then allow to rest for 1/2 hour before using.

2 Pit the dates and chop in a food processor. Add 1 tablespoon olive oil and the cinnamon.

3 Roll the dough to 1.5 cm (1/2 inch) thickness; cut into 6 x 10 cm (2 x 6 inch) strips.

4 Shape the date mixture into small rolls; place one on each strip of dough. Fold the dough over and seal the edges. Fry in hot oil until golden; drain on absorbent paper. In a sauce pan, dissolve the sugar in 1 cup water and the lemon juice; simmer down to a thick syrup. Cool to lukewarm and coat the *makrouds*.

STRUFFOLI

Honey Balls

400 g/3 ¹/₂ cups flour
5 eggs
1 tbsp lard
Salt
250 g/1 cup light honey
120 g/¹/₂ cup + 1 tbsp sugar
Peanut oil
150 g/6 oz candied orange
   and citron peel
Grated rind of 1 lemon
Assorted "sprinkles" for
   decoration
Pure alcohol

Servings: 4	
Preparation time: 30′	
Cooking time: 30′ + 1h	
Difficulty: ● ●	
Kcal (per serving): 1230	
Protein (per serving): 25	
Fat (per serving): 46	
Nutritional value: ● ● ●	

Make a well with the flour; blend in the eggs, the sugar, the lard, a pinch of salt, the lemon rind, and 1 teaspoon alcohol.
Knead the dough well, form into a ball, and allow to stand for 1 hour before using.
Divide into fist-size pieces; roll each into 1 cm (¹/₂ inch) thick ropes. Cut into ¹/₂ cm (¹/₄ inch) lengths and lay on a floured board.
Pan-fry the balls a few at a time in deep hot oil, ensuring they cook inside as well as out. Remove from the pan when golden; drain on absorbent paper and allow to cool.
Simmer the honey with a little water to make a golden syrup. Remove from the heat. Add the fried balls and half the diced candied fruit to the pan, stirring gently until the *struffoli* have absorbed the syrup.
Turn out on a serving platter and decorate with the sprinkles and the remaining candied fruit.

KARIDOPITA

Walnut Orange Cake

225 g/¹/₂ lb fine semolina
225 g/¹/₂ lb chopped walnuts
120 g/¹/₂ cup + 1 tbsp sugar
2 tbsp double-acting baking
    powder
¹/₂ tsp ground cinnamon
¹/₂ tsp ground cloves
Orange juice
Cognac
Olive oil

For the syrup
125 g/¹/₂ cup + 1 tbsp sugar
1 small jar apricot jam

Servings:	8
Preparation time:	25'
Cooking time:	45'
Difficulty:	● ●
Kcal (per serving):	650
Protein (per serving):	96
Fat (per serving):	8
Nutritional value:	● ● ●

1 Preheat the oven to 190°C/375°F. Grease a 22 cm diameter (9 inch) cake pan with olive oil. In a bowl, mix the semolina, the nuts, the sugar, the baking powder, and the spices. Add 12 tablespoons orange juice and 6 tablespoons cognac. Use a whisk to incorporate 12 tablespoons olive oil, a little at a time. Pour the batter into the cake pan and bake for 35 minutes or until a knife inserted in the center comes out clean.

2 While the cake is baking, prepare the syrup. Place the sugar with a little water in a saucepan; heat very slowly to boiling and allow to simmer imperceptibly for about 10 minutes. When the cake is done, remove from the oven, pour the syrup over it, and allow to cool. In the meantime mix the apricot jam with about 15 tablespoons water and simmer over very low heat. Spread over the cake and serve.

KIBRIZLI

Almond Cake

150 g/¹/3 lb fine semolina
180 g/³/4 cup sugar
120 g/¹/4 lb shelled almonds
1 tbsp double-acting baking
    powder
5 eggs, separated
Grated rind of 1 lemon
Salt
Sesame seeds
Olive oil

For the syrup
Juice of 1 lemon
Honey

Servings: 4	
Preparation time: 40'	
Cooking time: 50'	
Difficulty: ●●	
Kcal (per serving): 711	
Protein (per serving): 29	
Fat (per serving): 27	
Nutritional value: ●●●	

1

2

3

The eighteenth-century mosque of Urfa, in southern Turkey.

4

1 Beat the egg yolks with the sugar until creamy, blend in the grated lemon rind, the farina, the finely ground almonds, the baking powder, and 1 cup water.

2 Beat the whites with a pinch of salt until stiff and then gently fold them into the yolk mixture.

3 Pour the batter into a greased round baking pan lined with paper. Sprinkle the top with sesame seeds and bake at 180°C/350°F for 45 minutes.

4 Ten minutes before the cake is done, heat 3 tablespoons honey and simmer for 4 minutes. Remove from the stove and blend in the lemon juice. Pour the syrup over the cake. Allow to cool before removing from the pan.

BAKLAVA
Pistachio Cake

8 sheets phyllo dough
(or very thin puff paste)
(160 g/7–8 oz)
350 g/3/4 lb shelled
pistachio nuts
100 g/7 tbsp butter

For the syrup
150 g/²/₃ cup sugar
1 lemon
Orange blossom water

Servings: 4-5	
Preparation time: 35'	
Cooking time: 1h + 10'	
Difficulty: ● ●	
Kcal (per serving): 818	
Protein (per serving): 24	
Fat (per serving): 70	
Nutritional value: ● ● ●	

1 Arrange 4 sheets of dough in a buttered baking dish. Melt 70 g/3 oz butter and brush it over the dough.

Cover the dough with the chopped pistachio nuts and then put the other sheets of dough, each brushed with melted butter, on top. Bake at 170°C/350°F for 35 minutes, then raise the temperature to 210°C/400°F and continue baking for 10 minutes more.

Dissolve the sugar in 2 cups water and the juice of ¹/2 lemon; simmer until the syrup thickens. Add 2 tablespoons orange flower oil, cook 2 minutes longer, and remove from the stove. Let cool.

When the cake is done, pour the syrup over it and cut into lozenge-shaped pieces.

ZEPPOLE

1 Boil the rice in the milk until soft. Remove from heat and allow to cool. Beat in the flour, the sugar, the crushed cinnamon, the yeast, and the orange peel. Mix well until the dough is smooth and dense; leave to rise for 2 hours.

2 Spread the dough 2 cm (1 inch) thick on a cutting board, and cut into strips about 2 cm (1 inch) wide. Fry in deep hot oil. When the zeppole are golden brown, drain and dust with confectioners sugar.

400 g/2 ^{1}/4 cups rice
120 g/1 cup flour
100 g/7 tbsp sugar
2 cups milk
15 g/^{1}/2 oz compressed yeast
1 tbsp finely-grated orange
    peel
Cinnamon, 1 small piece
Confectioners sugar
Vegetable oil for frying

Servings: 4	
Preparation time: 40' + 2h	
Cooking time: 45'	
Difficulty: ● ●	
Kcal (per serving): 888	
Protein (per serving): 14	
Fat (per serving): 30	
Nutritional value: ● ● ●	